ISBN-13: 978-1502344182

ISBN-10: 1502344181

Lasciate ogne speranza, voi ch'intrate

WHERE ARE MY PANTS?

A must-have book in every toilet.

NIKHIL KUMAR

To Mansi

But tell me, did you sail across the sun?

Did you make it to the Milky Way to see the lights all faded,

And that heaven is overrated?

Table of Contents

An Apology To Begin With

You bought the book, didn't you? I pity you.

At the outset, I'd like to apologize for the contents of this book. This isn't your average blog-turned-into-book book. This book is rife with the most unspeakable forms of humor known to man. There is excessive swearing throughout these pages – very colorful, if I say so myself – and there is an abundance of toilet humor. Yes, I am ashamed to say that I have written things that make me come across as a narcissistic, chauvinist pig who's constantly farting.

I sincerely apologize. I live and let love. Most parts of this book were written long ago, when I was still a young idiot, trying, like so many others, to find my place in the great circus of life. I have grown up now (to an extent) and I no longer consider my views worthy of an audience. In fact, I'd strongly urge you to use this book as a door-stopper or to balance your lopsided tables. The reason I call this book a must-have in a toilet is for emergencies, when you run out of toilet paper.

I deserve punishment for the things I've written over the years. I am truly repentant and I hope the collective curses of everyone who reads this book is a start. I have created email IDs for all your feedback, which I have categorized as thus:

1. **Death Threats** can be sent to deaththreats@mirrorcracked.com
2. **Curses** can be sent to curses@mirrorcracked.com, and lastly,
3. **Suicide Tips** can be sent to killyourself@mirrorcracked.com

I am not kidding. These email IDs exist. Please make use of them, as I'm sure you'll feel the need to write to me once you've read the book.

This book is not for people who are under 18 years of age. This has to be strictly enforced.

This book contains some of the more colorful posts that I've written over the years on my blog – *MirrorCracked*.

If you haven't heard of it, then you are lucky. The blog was started in early 2008 and, either due to the nature of the articles or the nature of the people who read these articles, the blog became moderately famous for a very short time. I foolishly thought I'd reached the pinnacle of my glory and stopped writing. The ignominy of my blog's downfall taught me a very valuable lesson – two, in fact. Firstly, I learned to wear pants at all times. Secondly, I swore to never take things for granted. I had written unspeakable crap for five whole years and all the people who used to read it and laugh at it (or at me) grew up and moved on. I was left holding my metaphorical balls in my hand. I was humbled and I crept into a little hole under a rock and stayed there for the next three years.

The decision to publish this book was borne out of an idea that came to me when I was on the pot. I shit you not. I sat there wondering about the idea until my butt cheeks ran cold and shivered. I started reading the blog from the beginning and after a whole week of walking around in shame and hiding my head under a paper bag, I decided that it was time to re-inflict this disease upon the world.

This is my repentance. I need to be flogged in public and thrown in jail for the things I've written.

About The Posts

If you are smart enough, you'll notice that there are very subtle yet distinct changes in the writing style as you go through the book. I've intentionally arranged the posts in this book in an order that will make you love me first, then raise your eyebrows, then frown a little and finally, hate me with a vehemence.

Most of these were written between 2008 and 2012, and if you come across a reference that seems anachronistic, I apologize. I urge you to bear with me and continue.

If you aren't familiar with India, its people, its history, its current affairs and its politics, then, first of all, I envy you. Secondly, I have tried to insert little footnotes wherever possible to make sure some references aren't lost on you.

I love you, and I'd hate to see you get confused when I'm spectacularly butt-fucking Bollywood.

There is no central theme to these posts – all of them are randomly written, about random things that randomly exist by themselves. I've tried to group similar posts together for ease of comprehension and to provide a semblance of continuity because I'm a good guy.

According to me, the best way to get through this book is to read one article per poop session. I've found it to be an exceedingly useful way, because you can wash your hands after the deed (reading) and it also gives you an opportunity to throw it in the trash if you don't like it.

#1: Thanks For All The Spit

There comes a time in every guy's quotidian life when he questions himself thus:

1. Who am I?
2. What am I supposed to be doing? AND,
3. Where are my pants?

I did this yesterday and realized that I could answer two-thirds of the above questionnaire and felt very happy about myself. Just because I am in a good mood, I will share my responses with you.

Who am I?

A mildly confused, over-ambitious, relatively ignorant (I ignore my relatives), slightly overweight, extremely shortsighted, creatively challenged, socially active, coffee-guzzling, beer-loving, nicotine-abusing, technologically superior Neanderthal, working in an advertising agency. I wear worn-out clothes to work. My clients like me and the media is noncommittal, but I'm sure they like me too. I care deeply for a few people and for a few people, my care runs shallow.

What am I supposed to be doing?

Apparently, I am supposed to be working hard, trying to pretend that I know what I am doing. I accomplish this task with a positive nonchalance. I am supposed to be wrapping up the day's work early, today being a Friday. I am supposed to be thinking of newer pick-up lines for the sweet girl who thinks I am being serious when I say I like her a lot.

Where are my pants?

I have no idea. Someone stole my pair of jeans yesterday, when they had been hung out to dry. The only reason I had washed them in the first place was because someone spit on them. Yup, you read it right. Someone fucking spit on them.

Sleep-deprived and stuck in traffic at 8.oo in the morning on my way to work, I was wondering how a day could begin any worse. Just when the thought crossed my mind, I heard a man cough, clear his nose noisily, take a deep snort and spit out a major blob of sputum. It so happened that this environmentally-conscious citizen was sitting at a window seat of a crowded bus and that window just happened to be right where I was standing. The blob of sputum landed on my left leg, just above the ankle and splashed its thick drops of goo all over my shoes, forcing me to lose my temper, scream at that guy, show him the finger and call him a 'fuck-headed fucker.'

I returned home, put the pants in the washer, changed my shoes and came to work late. I went back home at night to discover that someone had stolen the pair of pants. I pity whoever stole them.

Thanks for all the spit, you fuck-headed fucker.

#2: Thirty & Me

At precisely 42 seconds past 5.30 this evening (on Aug 20, 2014) the Earth will complete its thirtieth revolution around the Sun with me on it. I have spent the past four hours reading about what it means to people when they exit their twenties.

Turning thirty is supposed to be a big deal, an achievement of sorts, having survived tsunamis, earthquakes, riots, murderers, diseases, ninja assassins and of course, traffic. It is also supposed to signify the fact that I've officially grown up and cannot rely on my youthful ignorance as an excuse when I screw up. I am supposed to be responsible, financially and emotionally stable, be able to hold down a job for more than three months and not throw boogers at passersby. I am not supposed to scratch my balls in public and have random fits of paranoia causing me to run down the road naked, dodging invisible aliens. I am supposed to be mature enough to realize the difference between right and wrong, morals and immorality, black, white and grey, and most importantly, coffee and tea.

I am supposed to start leading a healthier lifestyle – no more smoking, no more drinking binges and definitely no more weed. I am supposed to drink lots of water and work out regularly to ensure that my first heart attack happens only three decades from now.

I am supposed to be a strong pillar of support for my parents, be able to provide a good quality of life for my wife and be a responsible role model for my younger brother. I am supposed to be mentally strong to deal with the real world and I am not supposed to get depressed with the fact that I am growing old and am one year closer to death.

When I look back on the things I've done during the past three decades, I am surprised at the level of ignorance, insensitivity and intolerable cruelty that I have exhibited at times. I am also surprised at some of the intelligent decisions I've taken, something I was not sure I was capable of.

I've alienated people, I've infuriated those who love me and I've driven others to murderous rage. I can think of people who would put a bullet through me right now given the chance. I can think of people who would walk past me on the street and pretend to not recognize me. I can think of people who would smile at me and stab me in the back with the metaphorical knife when I turn around. But I can also think of people who would love me unconditionally and take me in as a part of their family. I can think of hundreds of people who would still acknowledge my existence without any animosity.

In a world filled with hate and anger, where people are being slaughtered each minute, the fact that one insignificant boy in Bangalore has grown up and turned thirty should not make a difference. But when I look at the journey I've been through to get here, I am overwhelmed. I am moved to tears at the kind of experiences I've had – the good, the bad and the ugly ones.

We all have fantastic experiences in our lives every day. Each moment of joy we experience means so much to us and it's hard to imagine hordes of such people being killed. Millions of dreams and hopes being crushed every single minute by people pursuing theirs. I ask myself if it's all worth it. Is it worth having a really 'happy' birthday when there is so much grief all around us? Or maybe, these tiny sparks of happiness keep the world turning.

We are all allowed meaningless rants straight from the heart, once a year. Today is my turn. As I see the clock inch closer and closer to the hallowed hour, I am filled with a little hope about hope.

#3: Message In A Bottle

Her memories still haunt me sometimes. It has been half a decade since I last told her that I loved her, and it has been less than a year since she told me to die a painful death. It's strange how the heart works – it seeks out the unobtainable and covets it. I sometimes lie awake at night thinking about her face, her smile, her lovely hair, her scent, her eyes – and feel this incredible amount of pain coursing through every sinew, blaming myself for what happened and wondering what might have happened if things had turned out differently. I reach out to touch her lips and clutch at thin air.

I have caught myself wondering, at times, whether she were the pinnacle of my existence. Whether everything I've done since she left, everything I've achieved or failed to achieve, all the adulations and the accusations that came after her, were just insignificant grains of sand on a beach. I have caught myself, at times, going through all those mails and letters we wrote to each other back then, expressing our undying, everlasting, unconditional love for each other. Maybe I was too young to realize what love really was. Or maybe I was too stupid to believe in its idealism.

I don't know where she is, I don't know what she is doing right now. I don't know if she is married, has kids, is working somewhere or studying something. I don't have her email ID. I definitely don't have her phone number. She doesn't follow me on Facebook, Myspace or Twitter. And I don't have her on any of my IMs. If it weren't for the old emails and letters that I'd saved, it's as if she does not exist. As if she had not existed in the first place. Someone as pure and as beautiful as her must have been ethereal, a figment of my imagination.

Just in case, hoping against hope that she is out there somewhere, and hoping that she can read this, all I want to say to her is that I do understand what love really is. This is probably my message in a bottle for her. I am keeping my fingers crossed and I hope that it gets picked up. I remember those days quite clearly. I remember those days so clearly that I wish things were that simple again. I wish life had not gotten in our way. I wish life would have remained so completely musical.

#4: Sliver

"No one cares when a clown cries..."

–Joan O'Brien
(1972, *The Day The Clown Cried*)

The clown stood in front of the mirror, leaning one hand against the wall. It was late in the night and the tiny incandescent bulb above the mirror did its best to drive out the lengthening shadows. He looked at his reflection, his alter ego, his image that wasn't true, and sighed. *This is not me*, he told himself. *I am not someone who gives up. I've been making people laugh ever since I can remember and now, in a matter of one week, I've seemed to slip.*

He shook his head and broke his train of thought. The make-up on his face was fading after a hard day's work and he could feel the tiredness in his legs creeping upward. He knew that come tomorrow, he would forget all his insecurities and go about his routine as if nothing were wrong. He knew, therefore, that this was the only time he could devote to some soul-searching. The tiredness could wait.

"You're desperate," someone had told him. "You are clutching at straws and hoping that people would laugh at your inane attempts at humor. You have lost your touch."

He cringed when those words played back in his head. He looked back at all those times when he felt genuinely satisfied about the quality of his work; he knew that he could manage to keep his audience enthralled come what may, and he had done it, time and again, over the past five years. And now...

And now, in a matter of a week, he had had three lousy performances and one no-show and he realized it a bit too late. Reviews started pouring in, and bouquets were replaced with brickbats. One member of the audience had walked out in the middle of the show, something that had never *ever* happened before. He had to pull up his socks or give up trying to make people laugh.

"I'm not someone who gives up," he told his reflection in the mirror. "Tomorrow will be a better day."

He splashed cold water over his face and closed his eyes, allowing the slight breeze to wash over him. His skin felt the heat of the day evaporating and his mind relaxed a bit. As he switched off the light and plunged the room into darkness, a tiny sliver of light from a street lamp forced its way through the half-open window, kissed the small imperfection on the mirror, and shone with an unexpected brilliance, reflecting a thousand times within the crack, causing a mosaic of light and glass.

The clown did not notice the mirror cracked with shards of light as he pulled the sheets over himself and fell into a dreamless sleep.

#5: The Storyteller

What's so special about having a blog? Is it the "cool" factor or is it the fact that having a blog allows us to meet new people every day, read their thoughts, views and opinions and comment on them? Do chicks dig bloggers? Or does sitting in our rooms, when the sun's bright and the birds are calling out, and punching out random thoughts into an online journal, a pack of cigarettes handy and an open pack of chips, get us high?

For me, personally, I think it's more to do with the fact that I've been cursed with an insatiable desire to write, to tell stories through the keyboard, that makes me blog daily and twice on Sundays. I do it religiously, and I don't really get bothered when I open my dashboard and see that there have been no new recent visitors. I'm sure that someday someone will read these lines and think, "Hmmm, he sounds nice enough."

But then again, that's not all. I think, for everyone who blogs, it's that innermost desire to tell their story to the world that's making them write it. There's a storyteller in every one of us. We need to just let him/her out and express those desires, explore those plots and give life to those characters trapped in our imagination.

Blogging isn't enough. We need much more. But then, maybe this is just me.

#6: The Nail Polish Scenario

There's a rat trapped in a maze, cornered by walls on three sides and a hungry cat on the fourth. The rat doesn't want to be there. It doesn't like the whole idea, but it is, unknowingly, a player in a sick game of sadism played under the auspices of scientific research. What does it do?

The rat knows that it has no chance against the big hungry cat. It can't scale the walls and it can't dig its way out. Simply put, it is well and truly screwed. Its life flashes before its eyes – those sweet, tender moments it had spent with its mother; those sweet, tender pieces of cheese that the human in the white coat had fed it; those sweet, tender minutes it spent with the pretty albino rat in the next room; those sweet, tender spots in the corner where it was cornered, where the temperature was just right and where it would have liked to curl up that night and dream of sweet and tender pieces of cheese if it weren't for the hungry predator smacking its lips and looking on in quiet amusement at the panic on the rat's tiny face. So, the rat makes a drastic decision.

Darwin was right – the fittest survive. The rat, trapped and helpless, proves to be fitter than the cat. The cat doesn't know and probably doesn't realize that for the rat, this is the last chance, the last stab at a chance to live, the desperation move. The cat is blissfully unaware of the fact that it has been the subject of study in a ground-breaking technology – one that renders cats slow in their reaction times.

The rat rushes forward towards the cat, with all the speed it can muster, and the cat looks helplessly on, as the seemingly suicidal rat slides through its feet and runs away from the corner, away from him, towards freedom and a well-earned piece of tender cheese. The cat doesn't quite understand how this happened. It stands there, looking at the empty corner, still not being able to comprehend the fact that the rat isn't there anymore. It blinks and looks around stupidly, trying to make sense of it. *It must have been that strange milk that tasted like nail polish, which the human fed me earlier*, it thinks. *I must be more careful next time.*

The rat, on the other hand, is on cloud nine. It begins to feel that it has superpowers and that it can outrun any cat. It smiles broadly as it bites into the piece of cheese. *What a strange taste*, it thinks, as it licks its paws. *Almost like nail polish.*

#7: How I Met Your Mother

The year 2030: Kids, have I ever told you the story of how I met your mother? No? Well, sit down, shut up and listen. No, you can't go and pee now. This story's important. Listen up.

The year 2010: There I was, sitting in the small, cubbyhole office, trying to be something I'm not, and all of a sudden, a wave of sleepiness forced itself on me. I don't think it was the heavy breakfast or the fact that I had slept for just a few hours last night, but I think it was a realization that I was twenty-six years old and I didn't have any discernible achievements to talk about. True, I had written a couple of books, and true, I had done a bit of traveling and dabbled with a lot of jobs, but I was twenty-six, single and stranded without any life goals to look forward to.

Monday, the 28th of June was an eye-opener for me.

She walked into my life with a sweet little smile and a lot of hope. I walked into hers with an upset tummy and lack of sleep. We clicked instantly. It was a day I can never forget.

Now that I think about it, I'm sure it was the heavy breakfast, because as she walked into the room with a handful of papers for me to sign, I burped loudly, causing her to shriek and throw me a look that seemed to say, "Ugh! Disgusting." She followed up that look with the words, "Ugh! Disgusting!"

I apologized and got down to talking to her about the day's work. I told her what needed to be done and I told her that I'd be leaving the organization soon. She looked shocked. Maybe at the ease with which I had slipped that last news in.

"Are you fucking kidding me? You can't leave! Who's going to do your work!?" she demanded.

I shrugged and said, "I'm sure you'll manage better than I can. Or they'll find someone to replace me. Either way, I'm outta here. All the best."

After twenty minutes of anger, pleading and threats, she realized she couldn't convince me not to quit. I didn't know why she was trying so hard. So, after a few futile attempts, she turned on her charm and said seductively, "But who will I flirt with?" and batted her eyelids in that sexy way that turns men on, and leaned on my desk, thrusting her very generous boobs at me. I instantly had the most massive hard-on ever. I gulped and made appropriate noises, trying in vain to look away.

(Author's Note: I have a massive hard-on now, while editing this. Damn!)

No kids, I'm not saying your mom was a slut. No, she was very sexy, and at that moment, I almost regretted my decision to quit. But sanity prevailed, and I did quit after a week. I started missing her seductive charm at first, and about sixty-seven days later, I got over her completely.

I don't quite know what happened to your mother after that.

The year 2030: Until today, kids. I ran into your mother at the supermarket and she invited me over to lunch. I saw your dad too, by the way. That's why I am here, having lunch with you. Ok, you can go pee now.

#8: Cooking With Love

Author's Note: I'm a fantastic cook. I can cook almost anything. I once cooked a chicken dish so delicious that I got a room at a five-star hotel and spent the night with it.

Someone said that the food I cook tastes so good because I cook with love. I started wondering about that comment and this is what I imagined myself doing:

It was a hot, sultry afternoon and the sweat trickled down my skin in thin rivulets as I stood in front of the stove and watched as the oil in the pressure cooker heated. In slow, gracious movements, I reached out and picked up the packet of *jeera**. The packet felt tingly in my sweaty palms, like a frail body waiting to be loved delicately. I added a bit of the seeds into the hot oil, just a bit, and watched as they turned brown and started sizzling, giving out the most heavenly aroma, wafting slowly up to my nostrils and tickling my most sensitive senses.

I grabbed a pair of onions, one with each hand, and ran my fingers all over them, caressing and squeezing the soft mounds. I kissed them – softly at first, and then nibbled hard at the ends, biting them off. I slowly peeled away the thin outer covering of skin and ran them both under a stream of warm water. The steam rising off the onions and my hands as I washed them felt so sensual that it brought tears to my eyes. I picked up a clean, sharp knife and sliced the first onion cleanly in half. It was like cutting butter with a hot knife, as I made the gentle motions of dicing the onions, with some of its juice oozing out with each cut, in and out, in and out, in... and out...

I added the sliced onions to the oil in the cooker, and immediately, they started sizzling and moaning in pleasure as their cold bodies touched the hot oil, jumping around in ecstasy and turning brown with pleasure. I gently poked at them with a ladle and began stirring them, softly, thoroughly, ensuring that no stray piece of onion sticks to the side, clockwise first and then, counter, feeling them sauté in the warmth of the fiery stove. They soaked up the oil and were dripping wet after a few minutes, completely fried and waiting to explode all our senses as they touched our wet, hungry lips.

I spiced up the whole affair with a bit of *MTR Pulao Masala**, gently sprinkling the powdered essence onto the wet, oily core of love, and watched as the onions hungrily ate it up, soaking in the taste and the color and spewing out the amazing aroma of the spicy mixture. The smell gushed out in torrents and filled me up, filled up the whole room, the whole house, and, it seemed the whole world stopped and took in the fragrance. I continued my gentle stirring motions and after what seemed an eternity compressed into two minutes, I added a bowl of fresh green peas.

The little balls of green ran and hid amidst the forest of hot wetness and sizzled where they stood, adding their own little sensuality to the fragrance. The onions, the spices and the green peas danced together in a carnal dance, a threesome made to last, enticing my every sense, oozing with pleasure and moaning in the sizzling heat, fulfilling their destiny, filling each other up and completing each other.

After a few minutes of watching them playing out their desires, and when the moans and sizzles settled down, I added two cups of wet rice, washed and cleaned. The *Basmati**, angry at being left out of the party, took over the gastronomic orgy with a vengeance, and orchestrated the most breathtaking display of lust and it seemed to show the other three lovers just how it's done. The onions, the spices and the peas gave in to the Basmati's superiority and embraced the millions of tiny specks of white-hot love and didn't let go.

Four cups of water, three tablespoons of salt, three whistles on the cooker, and the orgy was complete. Completely sated and thoroughly exhausted after the incredible display of *kama***, I had *peas pulao** for lunch.

[18]

If you don't know what these terms mean, don't worry. It's the taste that matters. If you are really curious, Google them.

** *Kama Sutra, bitch!*

#9: Top Five Worst Dates Ever

I've been dating ever since I turned eighteen. To be more specific, this girl at school asked me out on my very first official date on my eighteenth birthday. It was the year 2002 and I was just about to embark on my engineering studies. And my eighteenth birthday happened to fall exactly one month and two days before college was scheduled to start. So, I was at home, settling down for a nice, quiet birthday on my couch with my favorite TV shows, when this chick – Samyukta – texted me.

Here they are, by popular demand, the top five worst dates I've ever been on.

Number Five: Samyukta was this tall, lanky chick from my school and she had had a crush on me. I wasn't always as handsome and charming as I am now, but back then, I apparently had secreted just the right amount of pheromones to attract her. I was also naive and didn't understand women that much. When I was younger, I used to run down the school corridors lifting up girls' skirts as they leant against the parapet and laughed at them. I was that stupid. So anyway, this girl texted me and asked me if I wanted to go out and have some ice cream. I agreed and we decided to meet at the local ice cream parlor around 5.00 in the evening. I had no idea it was supposed to be a date because I didn't know what dates were.

I walked up there at the appropriate time, met her and we both ordered cones. She wished me a happy birthday, talked about this and that and commented on my new shirt and my latest hair style (I hadn't changed my hairstyle since the day I was born). I nodded politely and commented on her dress and pointed out that her ice cream cone was dripping. I finished my cone in about eight minutes. I got up, washed my hands, said bye and walked home to watch The Simpsons, which was supposed to start at 5.30. I failed to notice that she was still sitting there with a half-eaten cone.

I never heard from her again. I recently came to know that she's married and is living in New Zealand with her husband. Oh boy.

Number Four: Imagine the ugliest woman in the world. Now, multiply that by a million. Yeah, that was the first and last blind date I ever went on. I paid 1,500 rupees for my pasta and her sandwich, and I paid more attention to the food and the ambiance in the French restaurant than her. I ran out of there as fast as I could and never called her again. She tried to, but I was always either "caught in a meeting" or "busy with some work" or "not in the city." Trust me, blind dates are probably meant for people who can't see.

Number Three: Of all the places, this happened in New York. She was a fellow member of BOOBS – Buffalo Organization of Bangalore Students – and I was fairly attracted to her. I wanted to ask her out but didn't know how to. Moreover, I was supposed to be in a long-distance relationship back then, which was very quickly going downhill. So, I asked her if she's ever been asked out on a date before. She said no. So I told her that I would take her out on a "dummy" date and show her exactly how it worked. Well, she fell for my lame excuse to buy her food and get her alone, and agreed.

We went out to this Indian restaurant in Buffalo called *Palace of Dosas*, ordered a couple of eighteen-dollar-*dosas* and had a pretty nice time. When I dropped her off, she thanked me for dinner, said that she'd try this *I'll-teach-you-how-to-date* routine on a guy she was interested in, hugged me, kissed me on the cheek, ruffled my hair and ran inside, leaving me scratching my balls in the knee-deep snow. Yeah, I never spoke to that boob again. Bitch.

(Author's Note: The Buffalo Organization Of Bangalore Students (BOOBS) had twenty-one dirt-poor students as members, including me, all of whom were fucking retards.)

Number Two: This happened in 2007, when I was... um, "between relationships." I had been single for a while now and my job was quite a nightmare, as usual. On a relatively easy Friday, I met a girl on Facebook in the morning, added her on IM, chatted with her through the afternoon, got her phone number by 4.00 in the evening, called her up, fixed up a coffee date for 6.00 the same evening, met her, had a wonderful time, dropped her back home and got the shock of my life when she asked me if I wanted to come up for a joint of the best weed ever.

My brain was confused – were Indian women supposed to be this direct? I was so surprised by her question that I couldn't quite recall if I had any condoms in my bag. A few seconds passed as we just stared at each other. I thought that she probably thought I was playing hard-to-get or something, when she said, "Oh come on. It'll be fun. I'm sure my boyfriend won't mind. He'll be at work. He works night shifts."

Yeah, I made an excuse, went home and blocked the weird one from my IM list. No matter how hot you are, if you invite me to your place for a "joint," and you mean it literally, I'm not interested. What the fuck was she doing on a date with me in the first place, if she had a night-shift boyfriend? I don't condone cheating in relationships.

Number One: Interestingly enough, the worst date I've ever been on involves two women and a guy. This happened very recently at Hard Rock Cafe, in Bangalore. I went in as one girl's boyfriend, turned single inside, became another girl's random kisser and walked out hand in hand with a homosexual guy who kissed me on the neck and told me he loved me. I'll spare you the details.

Author's Note: This Samyukta chick was crazy – if you do come across her, please don't tell her I told you so. She will hunt me down and kill me, but not before torturing me with ice cream cones.

[22]

#10: The City Of No Goodbyes

I could feel the stress coursing through my every muscle as I rode my bike back home through never-ending traffic, monstrous trucks belching black fumes of smoke right at my face and millions of people running around on the roads, darting in between the rushing cars and bikes and trucks without, it seemed, a care in the world. I had had enough. I was burnt out and I could feel it in every breath and every heartbeat. My arms ached as I finally pushed the bike up the incline to my house and parked it beneath the awning. I stood, stretched my back and burst out laughing.

There was a reason I laughed out that day. It wasn't very profound; strange, rather. I knew I would quit my job. I had made my mind up on the ride back home and I had had enough of being a needle in a haystack. I had had enough of being a software developer in a country filled with so many software developers that someone had once said that if you threw a stone into a crowd in India, you'd either hit a stray dog or a software developer. I had had enough. I was burnt out and I wanted out.

I took a long, hot shower and washed the grime off my body and stood there under the running water, leaning against the wall and contemplating what I'd do. It was 7.00 in the evening on a Friday and I wanted to unwind. Making my mind up, I put on a tee-shirt and a pair of jeans and hailed a cab.

"*Sports Bar*, Colaba," I said and leaned back against the soft leather seats, feeling the blast of the conditioned air on my face and closed my eyes with a blissful smile.

I saw her standing at the other end of the bar, nursing a beer and talking to a few friends. The *Sports Bar* in Colaba has a corner where people can play mock basketball and make fools of themselves, but I preferred the slightly more mature game of billiards. A beer in my hand and some spare betting cash can go long way in making a good evening better. I had just won my third table in a row, when I noticed her standing there. She was wearing a white dress that came up to her knees, billowing around them, and I couldn't help but notice her long legs and the pretty white shoes she wore. As I took my gaze up, I noticed her perfect body, the firm breasts, the slender neck, her heart-shaped mouth, her long lashes and her long straight hair that came up to her shoulders and did a poor job of hiding her smile – the smile which, even from that distance, made me want to reciprocate.

It is said that we are all born with a sixth sense, and that we can actually sense someone's gaze on us. Even in that crowded bar, even amidst the noise and the soccer cheers and the crazy yahoos, she sensed my gaze and turned to me. I stood there, leaning on my cue stick, holding a beer in my hand, and smiled at her. What happened next remains, to this day, my most memorable memory of the city that never sleeps.

It was back at my place, at 11.00 in the night, that we first kissed. Her lips were on mine in mid-sentence and there were no awkward pauses and no drum-roll as we drew closer, unbeknownst to each other. Her wet, tender lips were crushing against my rough ones, frantically trying to accomplish something in a savage battle for dominance; her tongue found mine with scary ease and wrestled savagely for the same unsettling prize. We were sitting on the couch, my hands in her hair, hers on my face and we kissed long and hard, and with no apparent end to the lip wrestling in sight, we groped at each other's clothes. I struggled out of my shirt, and she, out of her dress, while still kissing with a kind of otherworldly passion.

I managed to get out of my shirt and I fumbled with her brassiere. I unclasped it with one hand while fighting her panties with the other. Her hands found my trousers and forced them down. I broke contact with her lips and traced my way to her neck, still kissing and licking and sucking on the sweet, soft skin and she moaned with pleasure. She threw her head back and gasped as I cupped her breast with my hand and kissed her gently on the nipple. I could feel it harden in my mouth as I nibbled on it softly. She screamed in pure pleasure as I bit down hard, gripped my hair and tugged on them.

[24]

I entered her in one swift motion and she gasped. She looked into my eyes and I, into hers and we began a slow rhythmic dance of carnal proportions, with gasps and screams. We picked up momentum and soon we were hurtling along the tunnel of desire at breakneck speed and burst through the clouds of mist and emerged into the bright sunlit skies of satisfaction. We lay back on the couch, thoroughly spent, sweating and exhausted. She nestled her head under my chin and I could smell her sweet shampoo mixed with my coarse deodorant. Her hands closed around mine and we fell asleep there, on the couch, just as midnight struck the sensual city.

"Let's not say goodbye to each other," she whispered as she went to sleep. "Ever."

Two weeks later, when I had to leave Mumbai for the last time and move back to my home town, I tried to call her a few times. She never answered. To this day, I wonder whether if I had stayed back there, I would have had the chance to do something about this woman who had come into my life in a whirlwind of passion and shown me the best two weeks of my life, and disappeared without saying a word. I wondered about all the things that we had talked about and about all the things we didn't. I most vividly remembered the nights of intense passion, where we would turn into animals and feast on each other until we were both thoroughly satisfied. I wondered if she missed me.

To this day, we haven't said goodbye. Yet.

#11: Checkmate!

The White Queen stood facing the Black Bishop. They were three squares away, in front of each other, in a single file. The Queen was tempted to kill the Bishop, but realized that there were other forces acting. The Black Queen and the Black King were very near, one square apart, on either side of the Black Bishop, providing excellent protection and at the same time, harboring a threat to the White Queen. The White Queen was of a pure heart, unlike the three enemies facing her – they were dark and sadistic. She knew that if she didn't think rationally at this juncture, she would be killed and her beloved White King would be helpless.

She called out to her White Knight – her trustworthy adviser, her secret love, her Man among men – and asked him to help her. Ever the gentleman and always ready to lay down his life for his lovely Queen, the White Knight rode forward and in one brilliant move, stood in front of his Queen, defending her, and called out, "Check!" to the Black King.

The Black King was taken by surprise and the Black Queen could not believe her eyes. Where had the White Knight come from? Her respect for the Knight grew, but was overtaken by her hatred and anger. She had to protect her dark King at any cost, and in her anger, she misjudged the existing threat to herself. She asked the dark King to move back a square, and when he did, she realized her folly. In an instant, the White Knight was on to her; drawing his sword, he plunged it deep into her Black heart. She let out a horrifying scream as she lay dying on the battlefield. Her last words were, "White Knight, I salute you."

Turning to his lady love, the White Knight bowed. The White Queen had tears in her eyes. "You risked your life to save mine," she said.

"That, my lady, is my destiny," said the White Knight.

The White Knight now stood right next to the Black Bishop, who was quivering in his boots and had wet his pants just looking at the spectacular warrior standing next to him in all his glory. The Black King knew that his hours were numbered. He looked back into his camp and saw that his trustworthy assassin – the Black Knight – was still available. He called out to him, "Save your King, O Blackest of Black Knights!"

Heeding to his King's call, the Black Knight leapt into action, and in one spring, he landed next to his King and threatened the White Queen. The Queen looked helplessly at her White Knight. He just smiled at her and said, "The dark ones are going to lose, my Queen. We shall triumph."

He leapt high in the air and landed in front of his Queen and called out, "Check!" to the Black King again. The King could not believe it. He had overlooked such a simple maneuver. "Shit!" he cried, and moved to a square to his right.

The White Knight then looked at his Queen, at her lovely face, at her beautiful eyes and extended his hand. "Do you trust me, my Queen?" he asked.

"Of course, I do!" said the Queen. "Why?"

"Then take my hand and come to me. Move a step towards me, my Queen. Trust me."

She took his hand. She loved him more than anything else in the world and so far, he had saved her life thrice in three moves. She took a step forward and came to him.

The White Knight looked at the Black King and said, "Checkmate, asshole!"

Bollywood & Everything Wrong With It

Author's Note: Bollywood is the Indian film industry's self-anointed misnomer. A long time ago, when it was still legal to plagiarize and call it 'inspiration,' someone had the brilliant idea to shoot a movie whose plot was a direct rip-off of a Hollywood movie. The rip-off was so perfect that they even had actors who looked similar to the ones in the original movie. It could have easily been called the literal Hindi version of the movie.

This rip-off became so famous and raked in so much money that Indian filmmakers, as a whole, began to realize what a gold mine of ideas Hollywood was. It's been estimated that 75% of the Hindi movies released in India over the past 10 years have been rip-offs of Hollywood movies. In a country like ours where more than half the population think "Hollywood" is just Bollywood misspelt and almost no one can spell plagiarize, new breeds of rascals were born.

The funny thing is, people still watch these movies with religious fervor. It pisses me off to no end that Bollywood is supposedly the richest film industry in the world.

And I'm just sitting here masturbating.

#12: Bollywood: A Cynical Deconstruction

"Western philosophy has often used architectonic terms—metaphors of base and superstructure, foundations and edifices, and founding moments and founding fathers..."

- *Of Grammatology,* Derrida

The last Bollywood movie I saw was called *Sarkar Raj.* I saw this in the month of July, and it was a forgettable experience. I broke a self-imposed rule of Bollywood abstinence and watched the movie, shelling out an unbelievable amount of money for the late night show. Over time, Bollywood has churned out spectacular loads of garbage, and I find it amusing (and slightly disturbing) that the industry still exists and is the richest film industry in the world.

A few years ago, there was a sudden increase in "item numbers" in Bollywood, a low-budget version of underground soft porn, and this revolution kicked off probably the largest number of flops ever recorded in any film history. Of course, I wonder where the directors and producers find the time to make these movies while battling plagiarism lawsuits.

"Bollywood" – the very name is somewhat of a joke. What the fuck does it mean anyway? Dictionary.com told me that "boll" meant the pod of a cotton plant. Apt, don't you think so? Add to this the equally ridiculous *Sandalwood* of South India, and we have a lousy bunch of losers who want to make movies under the garb of originality, creativity and hope! *Sandalwood, for God's sake!*

[30]

Coming back to the interesting point of plagiarism, I'm sure one in every three movies has been lifted from its Hollywood counterpart. Isn't there such a thing as a copyright anymore? I think not. The films themselves are comparable in quality to the dirt in our belly buttons, and very rarely is a movie made that can be watched without cringing. And what's the deal with the bad spelling, anyway? Kkkkkompany*? Singh is Kinnnng*?? Give me a break!

Put together a bunch of washed-out actors and directors, throw in a round or two (or ten) of tequila shots, make them believe that they're Mankind's last hope and what they come up with is a screenplay like *Padmashree Laloo Prasad Yadav*! Yeah, that's a real movie. This 3-hour load of fragrant shit was a sensation among the less-sophisticated audience.

Whatever's been said and done, I know for a fact that it's going to take something really sensational to make me watch a Bollywood movie again. I've had enough of second-rate droll to last me a lifetime. Hollywood has its misgivings too. I'll save my rants about the world's second lousiest film industry for a later time.

Author's Note: A lot of film names in Bollywood have been atrociously spelt. This is the effect of numerology. Apparently the film will be a commercial success if the name has extra k's or g's. Fucking retards.

#13: Roam Shanti, Roam!

"He was a junior artiste. She was a star. For some dreams, one lifetime is not enough..."

The tag line of the movie should've been a clue. I missed it. And I'm still regretting it.

The movie *Om Shanti Om* was a bit of a shock to me, initially. I took a really long time to grasp the flow of the story, and the other people in the room were too busy laughing their asses off at the supposedly-charming antics of an actor called Shah Rukh Khan (SRK) on screen. The storyline was a bit too strange, to be honest. Rebirth and revenge may have been a great theme back in the *Mona Darling** days of Bollywood, but now?

To my dismay, I completely lost the story when the male protagonist (SRK) dies in a car accident and is reincarnated as another guy, who looks just like him. The female protagonist – Shanti (portrayed by an actress called Deepika Padukone) – on the other hand, dies in a fire and becomes a ghost. I was half expecting them to be zombies of some sort, and hoping against hope that Bollywood had finally entered the Zombie Movie Era. It was not to be. The movie had to be stopped at every song and explained to me by the others, who were, at one point, ready to throw me out into the cold.

In a scene where the new and reincarnated SRK is going around in the dark, burnt-down theater, searching for the bad guy who killed Shanti, what would have been really cool is the sound of a distant flushing toilet or a smiley face etched on the wall, or better still, the original SRK, who'd have died there popping out of the ground like a zombie. Whatever. I don't think it makes a difference – if you haven't seen this trash, I envy you.

Which brings me to my biggest question: If Deepika Padukone can come back as a ghost in the end, why couldn't SRK? So, the spirit of Shanti roams around in the dark theater for almost thirty years, waiting for the off-chance that SRK can be reborn. Waiting for the off-chance that the reincarnated SRK drags the bad guy back to the theater. Waiting for her revenge.

Roam Shanti, Roam! The world is your oyster. Don't forget to put the seat down once you flush.

*The "Mona Darling" age of Bollywood was perhaps the Golden Era for the film industry here in India. During the 80s and the 90s, the films were just as bad as the ones today, but people were a whole lot dumber because the Internet hadn't been invented yet.

#14: Show-Lay

Author's Note: this is one of those instances where a bit of background information is deemed necessary. "Sholay" was a very popular movie that was released a few decades back. It starred the famous actors (who are now demigods) Amitabh Bachchan and Dharmendra in the leading roles. The storyline isn't that important – one guy dies, the other gets the girl. There's an armless lunatic who runs the show and there's a bloodthirsty gangster who cuts off said lunatic's arms.

There's a girl, who rides a horse-drawn carriage and falls for the guy who doesn't die in the end. "Chal Dhanno!" when roughly translated into English, means "Come on, Dhanno! You can do it, you sweet fucker!" This is the girl's pep talk to her horse, who is perhaps the only intelligent character in the movie. If all this sounds alien to you and you are wondering what's going on, well, join the club. This is my re-telling of the classic tale:

He was twenty-four years old when they cut off his hands. Both of them. They chained his hands to two pillars in an abandoned quarry, stretched them out and slashed them off with a pair of pick-axes. Or maybe Samurai swords, I don't really remember. The man who cut off the hands was called Gabbar. And the soon-to-be armless man was called Thakur. No last name. At least, I don't remember it now. This is a story of an incident that took place close to eighty years ago, when I was still a kid, living in the remote village of Ramgarh, somewhere in the hills of South India. And this story is not for the faint of heart. I call this 'Show-Lay'.

To understand why Gabbar cut off Thakur's hands, we need to understand the men themselves. Thakur was a man who had an unswerving belief in the pornography industry. Back in those days, when owning a television was a luxury and condoms hadn't been invented yet, Ramgarh had a thriving adult movie industry, run by the brilliant marketing genius Thakur. At twenty-three, he was the youngest porn star in the world at the time, and perhaps the first. The only mistake he ever did was cross Gabbar's paths. He regretted that day for as long as he lived.

Gabbar, on the other hand, was a foot model. He had the most exquisite feet in the whole of India and multinational leather brands like Cows and Alli McFeet featured Gabbar in their advertisements. No one could pull off a pair of silver-studded brown leather boots like Gabbar could, and the most famous advertisement to this day, has seen Gabbar sporting the latest summer line of Cows, walking slowly on the Ramgarh rocks, with a leather belt trailing behind him. Women literally fell over themselves to worship the ground he walked on, and naturally, he had a huge female fan following. There were rumors, don't quote me on this one, that Gabbar had insured his feet for a whopping fifty rupees from accidental damage, sexual damage and gangrene. Yeah, gangrene – he never removed his boots. Ever. Or so I've been told. And back in those days fifty rupees could buy you a ticket around the world with spare change left over to buy an island.

Long story short, Thakur slept with Gabbar's girl – the famous Basanthi. With a 'B'. We had strange names back then. Basanthi was famous all over South India for her, er, horsing around. Yeah, there's no better way to put it. She used to ride anything that moved and she loved her hooves. I mean, boots. She became so attracted to her stud Gabbar that she had a very special nickname for him – Dhanno. I don't know what that means, and rumor has it that they liked to play rough – with whips and restraints and a lot of screaming. Her ecstatic cries of *"Chal, Dhanno!"* reverberated through the village at night. And we all knew that Gabbar was one lucky cowboy.

So, this bastard Thakur not only slept with her, but made a movie out of it and it was called *"Basanthi ka Dhanno"* starring a drugged-out and subservient Basanthi and himself. Gabbar lost his mind when he came to know, and chased down Thakur through the hills, caught up with him

[35]

and cut off his hands. He was still wearing boots. From that day on, Thakur made it his life's ambition to take revenge on Gabbar, to put him behind bars and probably, strip him of his boots for good. He vowed never to smile until he achieved this. So, he hatched a plan – a plan so brilliant and so daring, that all of us village folk were astounded at the simplicity and the high projected success rates. We hoped he would succeed not because we liked Thakur, but because the plan was so good that it deserved to succeed.

Thakur paid for and got two of the world's most famous adult movie stars from Italy – *Veeru* and *Jai*. I have changed their names because they are good men at heart and I don't want to soil their image. So, Jai and Veeru waltzed into town one fine summer afternoon and Veeru promptly fell into his assigned role – keep Basanthi "occupied" while Jai tries in vain to seduce Thakur's widowed daughter-in-law from his third wife, while at the same time, trying to piss Gabbar off by copying his moves.

Veeru and Jai succeeded in irritating Gabbar to such an extent that he forced Basanthi to dance on broken bottles as punishment for sleeping with Veeru, and he made the two studs watch until they couldn't take it anymore. By this time, Basanthi was getting pretty tired of Gabbar's antics and his penchant for extracting horrendous vendettas and she agreed to help Thakur in his nefarious plan. Thakur smiled to himself – his calculations had been right, and everything was falling into place perfectly. Just when he thought he was ready for the master stroke, things began to fall apart.

He had sent his manservant to fetch vegetables from the market around midday when he realized that his breakfast had been a bit too spicy for his bowels to process. He dared not go to the loo alone because he knew his weakness – he couldn't, you know, er, how do I put it? Well, he had no hands, so you get the idea. He waited and waited, jumping from one foot to the other, squirming in agony, when he spotted Jai sitting outside blowing on a er... a "mouth organ", if you know what I mean. Thakur sent the naked guy away and beckoned Jai inside and asked him the favor.

"Why can't you do it yourself? I was busy with the mouth organ. I have a few new tunes," said Jai, pulling out a strand of hair that was stuck between his teeth.

"I can't. I don't have to explain it to you," told Thakur, furious.

"The loo is right there. Why can't you go on your own? I am not cleaning anyone else's shit. I stopped doing that a long time ago," said Jai.

"Try to understand!" screamed Thakur. "I can't do it!"

Just then, there was a gust of wind that caught the blanket that Thakur always wrapped himself with and carried it away, leaving Thakur standing there in all his armless glory. Jai saw that Thakur was, well, crippled. He tried hard to keep a straight face at the sight of the old horny geezer with no hands, and helped him into the loo. Some people say that Jai slipped on a piece of soap in the loo, but others are not too certain about whether what he slipped on was a piece of soap or something else altogether. Whatever it was, he hit his head hard on the cast-iron sink and bled to death.

Veeru, in his alcohol-induced state of near-comatose stupidity, believed Thakur's story of Gabbar sneaking in the loo and killing Jai, and went off in search of the nefarious foot model. He found him hiding among the rocks, and promptly went on to beat the shit out of him. No puns intended. Thakur intervened at the last minute and ordered Veeru to stop killing the guy. He stripped the boots off Gabbar's feet and put them on himself – with a little help from Veeru. He stared at the cowering, sniveling Gabbar with bloodshot eyes and told him, "You took away my hands, now I take away your boots, Gabbar!"

"No!" screamed Gabbar.

"Give me these boots, Gabbar!" Thakur screamed like a rabid dog in heat, waving his boot-covered feet in front of Gabbar's face, taunting him.

[37]

"No!"

"Give! Me! These! Boots!"

"Aaaaaaa!"

"Aaaaa!"

And when both of them screamed "Aaaa!", the whole village heard them. It took us a while to realize that it wasn't another one of Thakur's porn movies, but the real deal. Gabbar never dared to wear boots again. In fact, he ran away and was never heard from again. Thakur lived to the ripe old age of forty before passing away in the middle of an intense 3-day marathon. No, not the running type, if you catch my drift.

Veeru and Basanthi lived happily ever after, being ridden and riding, respectively.

I grew up, moved to the city, lived my life to the fullest and now, I can barely remember my name, but this story of Ramgarh shall remain with me forever. Vividly. Someone should make a movie out of this or something. It's really an intriguing tale.

#15: Bollywood Does It Again

Or, more precisely, *Karan Johar** does it again. He has taken a clichéd plot, soon-to-be washed up actors, ridiculously lame jokes and unoriginal catch-phrases from How I Met Your Mother and dished out two-and-a-half hours of pure and unadulterated horse shit.

He calls this soporific, brain-damaging spiel *"I Hate Luv Storys"* – a phenomenon that I had the misfortune of watching last night.

Here's what happens in the 135-minute joy-ride from Hell:

(Relax & ignore the spoilers, you're not missing anything worthwhile)

There's this guy, see, who's disgustingly like Barney Stinson from HIMYM – he's against the concept of love and he wants to sleep with a new woman each night. He considers the age-old concept of love lame, and does not want any part of it. Ironically, he works as an assistant to a Bollywood movie director who specializes in just this sort of crappy movies. So, here ends the interesting part of the movie. Before it begins.

He meets a girl, who falls in love with him. He says he doesn't want to fall in love. I think he hides the fact that he's ridiculously and unbelievably gay, but that hasn't been shown in the movie. He rejects her advances – which is strange, because when he first meets her, all he's thinking of is how beautiful she is and how he can get into those pants of hers. Anyway, such contradicting plot lines are the backbone of this crapoweseome** movie.

[39]

And then, as with all the other slipshod Bollywood movies, the hero (or rather, the actor-playing-the-lead-role) realizes that he's lost his mojo and can't get it up with any other woman, and all he thinks about is this chick. So, he decides to fall in love lest he spend the rest of his 'manhood' making love only to himself and the ever-present girls-gone-wild video that seems to be playing on constant loop in his room. How bizarre.

He tell her that he loves her and now, it's her turn to bitch-slap him and walk away. Aww, the poor sod is all heart-broken but decides to stalk the chick all the way to New Zealand, in the hopes of scoring with her. But he realizes that the chick has agreed to marry some other loser named Raj, who wears atrocious shirts that look like something a cat dragged in, pooped on and dry-humped your neighbor's Barbie doll on. So, our hero (or rather, the loser-who-plays-the-actor-who-plays-the-lead-role) decides to be generous and let her be taken by his nemesis.

And, just when he seems to settle down in his head, resigned to his fate of returning home to live with his insanely liberal mother (who, it seemed, would appreciate the beauty and charisma in anything from a sordid threesome to a full-blown monkey orgy) and marry some girl that she's chosen for him, fate delivers the knock-out punch – his flight gets delayed and he realizes that he's not in a Bollywood movie but rather in Paulo Coelho's Alchemist, interpreting each and every coincidence as a 'sign' from the *ooparwala* (literally translated to *the one above*. Doesn't mean your overweight upstairs neighbor who can't keep it down, though. It's a way of referring to God.)

He runs back to the chick, tells her he loves her, and this time, amazingly, she says yes. Apparently, by this time, she has realized her mistake – she did not want to spend the rest of her life smelling of cat poop. Or maybe she realizes that the movie's run time is almost over and she can't delay it any longer.

They hug, they kiss, the movie ends and the audience pukes.

There you have it – fresh from Karan Johar's box of unbecoming movie ideas that he cooked up while getting drunk with four guys from Canberra who took turns in showing him exactly how handsome he is.

[40]

Well, serves him right. Inox and PVR theaters all over the country are smelling of vomit and they have decided to shut down for a day to clean up the mess, under the pretext of the *Bharat Bundh**** today.

#16: Deconstructing A Movie Review: Haunted

Two nights ago, my dreams were haunted by images of a crazed piano teacher trying to rape a moderately pretty woman. I didn't understand what this meant until I realized it was a premonition of something far more horrifying. I went to see the movie "Haunted" at Inox and to my surprise, the story line was similar to my dream. Okay, I just made that up. I did not dream any rape scenes. I was just trying to make this review a bit more interesting, because the movie has absolutely nothing to offer.

I won't give any statutory spoiler alerts because you don't need it. The movie's storyline, plot, twists and turns can be predicted with pin-point accuracy after watching the first five minutes.

So, here's the deal: In 1936, a sex-hungry piano teacher lusts after his student, who's a moderately good-looking dame. He tries to rape her one fine day, and ends up getting hit by a candle-stand on the head and dies. (By the way, when he dies, he falls on her boobs and gets a good look at them). So, this guy dies and comes back as a ghost and finishes what he started. He rapes the chick for a week (yeah, ghosts can rape women, apparently) and in humiliation, the girl kills herself. Then she becomes a ghost. But the fun is just starting – *his* ghost keeps raping *her* ghost in the house for 80 years. Yeah, it's a lot of rape.

Eighty years later, the protagonist of the movie arrives in town to sell the house and realizes there are two ghosts in there, playing hanky-panky. He sees a photograph of the chick and falls in love with her (obviously) and decides to "set her spirit free". Whatever that means.

So, get this, he goes back in time! Yeah, he goes back in time to 1936 and tries to prevent the girl from killing the pervert pianist. Instead, in a fantastically typical Bollywood twist, he fails to do so. Astonishing! Anyway, he decides to tackle the rapist ghost himself and does all sorts of feats worthy of a Jason Bourne Award for Unbelievable Acts of Physical Endurance, seeks help from a church and a mosque, and kills the ghost. Yeah, he *kills* the ghost in the end.

How does he do it? Well, I think you should watch the movie for that. Why should I be the only one wasting money on such pristine crap?

In the acting department, the protagonist does not do justice to the ridiculous direction and the paper-thin plot. He looks as if he is about to fart all the time, he runs like a girl on dope and dances like a chimp on dope. The chick who plays the lead role – the ghost who gets raped all the time – has nice boobs and that's just about all I can say about her acting skills.

The sound effects are good enough to keep you from falling asleep, with timely crescendos and unnecessarily loud shrieks of the ghost getting raped. The movie, which had a lot of hype before its release, claiming that it's pushed Bollywood's horror genre to a new high, fails to live up to it. Every one of the ten people in the huge (empty) movie hall were testament to this fact.

It's definitely worth a watch, if you have two-and-a-half hours to kill and are bored in life and need some good *desi* entertainment. Else, I'm surprised the movie is still in the theaters.

[43]

The Adventures Of Hairy Potter

Disclaimer: Hairy Potter is my creation. It has absolutely nothing to do with the other one – the one you're thinking of. I have not stolen any ideas. Any resemblance to any characters in the series of stories you are thinking of is purely coincidental.

I swear upon the graves of my ancestors that the resemblance in names is in no way intended to cause harm to the author of the other series of stories you are thinking of.

I am a nice guy. Don't sue me.

#17: Hairy Potter And The Over-Ambitious Gall Stone

"I stirred from my sleep at around 8 in the morning. The sun streamed through the window and made my hairy chest glow a brilliant red. I looked around my room and saw bits and pieces of pottery lying as they had been the night before – haphazard and lacking order. My flowing beard got caught under my feet as I stepped off the bed and I couldn't prevent my head-long fall. The ground rushed up and I hit my head on the hard red-oxide floor and I passed out.

"When I woke up a little later, I was surprised to find that the fall had driven my brain against the walls of my skull and opened up a new dimension. I was blessed with superhuman bladder control. I haven't pee'd for two weeks now..."

"Whoa, wait. Hold on a minute!" said the police inspector as he switched off the tape recorder. He looked skeptically at the strange man sitting in front of him – he was covered in hair from top to bottom; hair was flowing from every part of his body, and the inspector wondered if he was wearing any clothes.

"Are you telling me that your *beard* got caught under your *feet*?" asked the inspector incredulously.

"Yes, it's true," said the hairy man. "Please believe me!"

"It's hard to, but I'll let you go on, Mr – "

"Hairy. I'm a potter. So, as I was saying, I have superhuman bladder control."

"Ok," said the inspector. "Where does the Gall Stone come into the picture?" He didn't sound convinced.

"Ah, the Gall Stone," said Hairy Potter, and smiled...

In the dark recesses of Hairy's left kidney, there lived an Over-Ambitious Gall Stone. It wanted to break free from its confines and see the world. Unfortunately, Hairy's bladder movements were almost nonexistent now that he had superhuman bladder control. For a whole week now, the Gall Stone hadn't been able to move. Then, it made a drastic decision – it decided to break out of its prison.

Bladder control or not, the Over-Ambitious Gall Stone started digging a tunnel in the kidney in order to break free, without caring about the tremendous pain it caused Hairy. Hairy realized that he had to go check himself into a hospital to relieve himself of the pain. The doctors decided to operate and remove the Gall Stone.

As soon as the surgeon clutched the Gall Stone in his forceps and brought it out into the open, it squealed, "I'm Freeeee!" and jumped out and started rolling towards the door. No one could find it anywhere.

"So, I want you to arrest the surgeon for losing my Gall Stone. I wanted to store it and show it off to my friends. I told the doctor categorically to preserve the Stone. He didn't care about my wishes, and now, I want him arrested," said Hairy Potter.

The inspector switched off the tape recorder a second time and placed his hands on the table and leaned forward. He looked at the hairy creature in front of him.

"Sir," he said. "Do you think I'm fucking insane?"

Hairy was flustered. "What? Why?"

"Two weeks? You haven't pee'd in two weeks? *Get out before I arrest you for attempted suicide!*" he said. Hairy jumped up and moved towards the door, feeling scared and bit annoyed that the inspector hadn't even considered his Gall Stone issue serious.

"The toilet's on your left. Go do your business and go home, you fucking loony!" the inspector called out after Hairy.

After making sure that Hairy had left, the inspector dialed a number.

"Lord Wall 'de Fart?" he asked.

"Yesss," the voice hissed.

"I think we may have found it. The Gall Stone Who Lived..."

[to be continued...]

Author's Note: In the interest of educating the younger readers, gall stones are found in livers. Not kidneys. Hairy Potter is special. You're not. Go do your homework.

#18: Hairy Potter And The Chamber Of Cigarettes

The story so far:

(For the best experience, read this backstory while imagining dramatic music playing in the background. Maybe the music from the movie Speed. And imagine Morgan Freeman narrating this.)

Hairy Potter realizes he has been blessed with superhuman bladder control! He has an Over-Ambitious Gall Stone in his kidney that wants to break free! It finally manages to escape! Angry at the surgeon for losing his precious Gall Stone, Hairy Potter goes to the police and asks them to arrest the surgeon. The inspector is secretly working for someone named Lord Wall De Fart, and they both realize that they've been searching for the Gall Stone Who Lived, and now they are nearing their quest.

Will Hairy find justice?

Will the Gall Stone see the world?

Who is Wall De Fart and why does he want a Gall Stone?

Read on to find out...

Hairy was dejected. He was extremely depressed because of the way the inspector had treated him. He was sitting at the bar, drowning his sorrows in alcohol, oblivious to the strange stares he got from the other drunkards. Three cases of beer later, he realized that he had to relieve himself. He was startled because it was the first time in almost two weeks that he had had to pee. It was a momentous occasion.

He stumbled his way to the restrooms and in his drunken stupor, entered the ladies' restroom. He entered a cubicle, parted his hair carefully and started pee'ing. "Oh wow! That feels so good!" he screamed in pleasure.

*

Meanwhile, in the nearby town of Dips-Hit, a cloud of fart mysteriously floated in the corridors of an ancient house and made its way into a well-lit room. A strange thing was sitting on the only chair in the room – it was a creature with no body and yet, it had dark brown evil eyes. A bigger cloud of fart was enveloping the creature, and the cloud that had just entered, stood in front of its master and said, "I have come, master."

"What newssssssss?" hissed the fart-cloud-covered creature.

"The Gall Stone is in Sydney," said the smaller fart cloud.

"Ssssssydney?? How did it get there??" screamed the creature.

"I.. I don't know. I just saw the airline manifests this morning," said the small fart cloud, cowering in fear.

"Hmmm..." said the creature thoughtfully. "Under what name is it traveling?"

"O.A. Gall, your Fartness," said the smaller fart, now a little relaxed as its master's anger seemed to have ebbed.

"I sssseee. And what about Hairy Potter?" the creature hissed. The anger rose again, sending fresh shivers down the metaphorical spine of the smaller fart cloud.

"My sources tell me that Hairy Potter is dangerously close to discovering the Chamber of Cigarettes," said the smaller fart cloud slowly, fearing for its life now. Its master's anger was very dangerous.

[50]

"Whaaaat!?" screamed the creature as it sprang up from the chair. *"What nonsense is thisss?"* it yelled, as a thin, white hand emerged from the cloud, holding a gun. "I'll shoot you right here if you don't tell me how this happened. How did Hairy Potter manage to get so close?"

The smaller fart cloud was shivering and crying by now, and between sniffs, it said, "Please! Please don't kill me, master. One of my sources told me, I swear. It's true. I don't know how this happened. Please don't kill me."

"Get out," said the creature quietly and lowered the gun. "I have to think."

*

Half an hour had passed and Hairy was still going strong. He was creating patterns on the wall with his never-ending stream of urine, when finally, the flow reduced in intensity and gradually trickled down to a stop.

"Oh wow! Wow! Oh yeah!" he cried in satisfaction. As he reached for the flush handle, his feet hit something strange on the ground. Bending down, he saw a small metal ring with something carved on it. Curious, he picked it up and turned it around. It was a cheap metal ring, which anyone could pick up off the flea markets, but the inscription on the ring was quite stunning – it showed a toilet cubicle much like the one in which he was standing, and the flush handle in the carving had been pushed up, instead of down.

Hairy looked at the ring and then at the flush handle in his own cubicle. "Why not?" he said and pushed the flush handle up, instead of down. He could hear a strange rumbling noise somewhere beneath him and in a few seconds, something strange rose up from inside the commode, from the depths of the ground.

It was a small iron box, about two feet wide and two feet high, dripping wet and sitting on a metal platform of sorts, with the words, **"The Chamber of Cigarettes,"** written on them in a nice, flowing font. On the side facing Hairy, there was a hole in the center with the words "Insert Ring Here" written in a smaller font. Hairy put the ring in the hole. It fit perfectly and the lock clicked and the box swung open. He looked in and his eyes widened in surprise by what he saw inside.

There were two cigarettes, identical to each other, guarded by a small lizard-like creature. It was a common house lizard and Hairy picked it up by the tail and threw it down the drain. He then picked up the two cigarettes pocketed one of them for later and lit the other one. It was the best cigarette ever.

*

At that precise moment, the fart-cloud-covered creature let out a horrible scream – a scream of agony, pain and defeat.

"Hairy Potter! I will get you for this! Do not cross Lord Wall De Fart! Hisss!"

*

Totally oblivious to all these happenings, the Over-Ambitious Gall Stone was sitting in a bar in Sydney, munching on peanuts, totally enjoying its vacation. Two tables away, watching O.A Gall and nursing its beer, sat a small cloud of fart.

[to be continued...]

#19: Hairy Potter And The Barber Of Andaman

The story so far:

(For the best effect, read this backstory while imagining dramatic music playing in the background. Maybe the music from the movie Speed. And imagine Morgan Freeman narrating this.)

Hairy Potter, who's blessed with superhuman bladder control, finds an Over-Ambitious Gall Stone (O.A. Gall) in his kidney, which escapes its confines and runs away to see the world. Hairy is depressed over this fact and with the absolute indifference shown by the police in this regard, and gets drunk. He urinates for the first time in 2 weeks, and by mistake, stumbles upon the Chamber Of Cigarettes in the ladies' toilet. He smokes one of the cigarettes in the Chamber, and this does not go undetected by the elusive and villainous fart cloud – Wall de Fart.

Wall de Fart wants revenge on Hairy Potter for encroaching on his hidden Chamber. He also wants O.A Gall killed, for some strange reason, as yet undisclosed. He discovers that O.A Gall is in Sydney, and is keeping the Gall Stone under close surveillance.

Why is the Chamber Of Cigarettes so important to Wall de Fart?

Who is Wall de Fart?

Why is he so interested in Hairy and his Gall Stone?

Why is Wall de Fart a cloud of fart?

Read on to find out...

The reporter was a piece of shit. Literally.

He wrote for a newspaper called *The Daily Fart*, which had a readership of more than a million. So, he had *some* credibility. He sat in the dingy room, regretting his decision to come. He looked at the strange creature in front of him and felt fear flowing in his veins. He never should have requested this interview.

"You never should've come here," said Wall de Fart, staring intently at the reporter. "Why do you want to know my story so badly?"

"Well," said the piece-of-shit reporter. "You've always been something of a mystery to all the readers of *The Daily Fart*. I want to show them the man behind the cloud of fart. Is it true that your name has a literal connotation to it?"

Wall de Fart thought for a while before replying. "Your sources are good, I give you that. Ssso, let's talk about my background," he hissed. The reporter shivered.

"A long time ago, I was attacked by the greatest fart cloud ever known to man. The force was so great that I was hurled against a wall nearby and lost my physical body. Some strange phenomenon occurred and I acquired the cloud of fart as my body, and in the process, the greatest fart cloud died. I am proud of it. I became Wall de Fart."

"Hmmm... Right," said the reporter, trying not to sound insolent. "And the prophecy...?"

"Ah, the prophecy," said Wall de Fart. "There's a prophecy that predicts that I'll be killed by an abnormal phenomenon. Most of the abnormal phenomena in the world have already been "taken care of," if you know what I mean!" he said and laughed out loudly. "Now, only one such abnormality remains, but not for long. No one can defeat the greatest fart cloud of all time! Hissss!"

The reporter shook in his chair with fright. "And wh-what is this abnormality?"

Wall de Fart just smiled at him.

*

O.A. Gall finished his drink and looked around the empty bar. He was tired of Sydney. He wanted to go somewhere he could let loose and feel the adrenaline. He made up his mind. The next day, he boarded a flight to the Andaman Islands to go scuba diving. He did not notice the small cloud of fart hiding near the passport counters, as he passed it. The small cloud of fart made a single phone call and left the airport.

*

The Barber of Andaman was the greatest assassin known to the world. Er, I mean unknown, but known to the right people, and feared by the rest of the ignorant world. He was silent, swift and rarely made mistakes. He also charged 30% more than the other assassins, and never advertised in the Yellow Pages. He was a brute of a man, over seven feet tall, and strong as an ox. There was nothing he feared in the world. Yet, as he flipped his phone shut, he was pale and shivering.

*

Meanwhile, Hairy Potter decided to visit his God-Farter and ask him for advice. He felt really depressed, and the alcohol hadn't helped at all. He bought a flight ticket to his God-Farter's city and left the next day. Two seats behind him on the plane, sat another small fart cloud, watching Hairy and studying his every move. It flipped open a phone, sent a brief text message and switched off the phone, removed the SIM card, broke it in two and disposed of the phone.

*

O.A. Gall donned the wet suit, adjusted his breathing apparatus and plunged from the boat into the brilliant blue sea. As the first waves hit him, he knew it had been the right decision to go scuba diving. He felt a surreal calm sweep over him, and he felt weightless as he began to sink beneath the surface. He breathed the compressed air deeply and saw the amazing spread of marine life beneath him, and smiled for the first time since he had escaped from Hairy's kidney.

*

[55]

Unknown to O.A. Gall, the Barber had him in his sight. He adjusted the high-powered rifle and squinted through the lens, and found the tiny mass of The Over-Ambitious Gall Stone floating just beneath the smooth surface of the ocean. He gripped the barrel lightly, breathed deeply and put a finger to the trigger, and was about to squeeze the trigger, when someone screamed behind him. He jerked up in surprise but it was too late – the bullet whizzed from the gun, silently because of the silencer, and dropped harmlessly in the water.

The Barber was burning with rage when he turned around, but the anger disappeared when he saw who had screamed.

"Hi God-Farter!" screamed Hairy and ran up to the Barber and threw his hairy body around him. "Oh, I missed you!"

The Barber forced the tears from his eyes. "Hairy! Oh, Hairy! I missed you too! What are you doing here? How've you been?"

"I've been all right. I just needed someone to talk to," said Hairy as he released his God-Farter.

"Hairy, I believe we both are in very grave danger right now," said the Barber solemnly. "I just failed in my first assignment, and the man who gave me the assignment is not going to be happy about it. No one fails Wall de Fart..."

Hairy's eyes widened in surprise and shock as he heard the name, and felt the fear flood his body like darkness at dusk. He watched as the giant Barber fell to his knees and cried.

*

The stray bullet from the Barber's gun lodged itself in the ocean bed with sufficient force to stir up a few artifacts. Among the debris that had been disturbed, was an ancient coin with strange inscriptions on it.

O.A. Gall saw something floating up towards him from the depths, and saw the glint of sunlight on the object. He dived down and clutched the coin in his tiny hands and surfaced. Once on the boat again, he looked carefully at the coin. It had a strange cloud-shaped design etched on it, with the words, *"Ne pas péter de couchage sur le dragon"* inscribed around it. His French was sufficiently advanced to realize that this translated into, *"Do not fart on the sleeping dragon."*

For the first time in his life, O.A. Gall was afraid.

[to be continued...]

#20: Death Of A Legendary Warrior

Ladies and gentlemen, friends, fellow bloggers, distinguished colleagues, kids, addicts and all the random people who stumbled upon this book because of the keyword *sex*, please join me in a moment's silence to mourn the death of the greatest man ever known to exist.

Some may claim he never existed but I beg to differ. He existed in all of us, we all have a part of him and he was an integral part of all of us. He came out of nowhere and stole our hearts, made us laugh until we cried and then, without a warning, left us all and joined the other martyrs.

He was an icon. He was a legend. He was the warrior that I can never be. He gave me a reason to write about him, and now, I never shall. It gives me great sorrow to announce the death of Hairy Potter.

Last time we heard about him, he was somewhere in the Andaman Islands, trying to find meaning to his life and to all the unanswered questions that kept cropping up everywhere he went. Last night, he had an unfortunate accident while combing his hair – in a very delicate place – and inadvertently, he combed something that wasn't supposed to be combed.

Now, we will never know the answers to all those questions that haunt us day and night. We can never reveal the truth. Hairy was the only person strong enough to face the realities and now, he's gone. There was some talk that this was the handiwork of the elusive Wall de Fart, but nothing can be proved. I cried the whole night. I attended his funeral this morning – it seemed the entire world had come to see him off.

Even in death, he exuded that hairy confidence that filled us all with inspiration.

Rest in peace, Hairy. We will all miss you, my friend. I envied your bladder control and now, I envy your peace. Fight on, Hairy.

The Only Guides You'll Ever Need In Life

#21: The Dummy's Guide To The Basic Rules Of Blogging

So you think you know how to blog, do you? Well, if you do, then good for you! Sometimes, the ability to delude ourselves is an important survival tool. For all those unfortunate netizens who sit and stare with open mouths at blogs and wonder how it's done and for all those fortunate ones, who think they know how to blog, here's a must-have quick reference – **The Dummy's Guide To The Basic Rules Of Blogging.**

It's about bloody time someone taught us how to blog!

Rule 1: Eat

Before you even think of blogging, eat well. I suggest a couple of bowls of chicken soup as well. There is a scientific reason behind this and I don't want to go into the details. It has something to do with the ability to stifle a yawn.

Just take my advice – eat heartily, sit in front of the computer and open the blog engine homepage.

Rule 2: Logging In

You can use your own username and password or you could steal someone else's. It actually doesn't matter as long as you get in. There's a button that's usually present next to the password field that says "Enter" or "Submit" or "Log in" or, sometimes, very rarely, "Spank Me." Click that button. Congrats, you've just logged in.

Rule 3: Do A Tag

You'll never be recognized as a blogger if you write shit and don't do tags (or a meme, as it's called nowadays). Very few people know this, but the word "Tags" is an acronym – it stands for "Towards A Greater Sexlife."

The reasoning behind this would probably be the increasing amount of personal information that is being shared in each and every tag. (Oh, you wouldn't believe it, but I once did a tag in which I asked a beautiful woman to marry me. But that's just me. Different people reveal different things.)

So, beg, borrow or steal a meme, and do the tag. You'll be certified as a blogger.

Rule 4: Etiquette

Just two words: No Nudity!

Whatever you write, whatever you comment, whatever photographs you upload and display, please make sure that your nude photographs and descriptions are not among them. No one wants to know. No one cares.

Rule 5: Comment Policy

One of the main aspects of blogging is building good relationships with fellow bloggers. This can be achieved by visiting their site and leaving a scar comment on their article. This will force them to return the favor and voila! You've got a rudimentary blogroll! Now, don't repeat that again. A good blogger never replies to comments or retaliates in debates. A good blogger is always too drunk to do these things.

Rule 6: Logging Out

Finally, after everything is said and done, you may search your page for a "Log Out" button. This button is also, very rarely, called "Spank Me Again."

Go ahead. Blog! Show the world what you've got! Let me rephrase that – Show the world how creative you can be!

We don't want to break Rule 4, do we?

#22: The Dummy's Guide To Destroying Your Computer

Author's Note: This Guide is intended only for users of Microsoft Windows. If you are an Apple fanboy/fangirl, you have my sympathies. You've had it easy in life. You will never understand the struggles that every Windows user goes through. Windows users have become immune to hardship and heartbreak over the years. Windows builds character and makes us better people who are better prepared for all of life's disappointments.

Ah, so you somehow reached this page. Are you frustrated with your computer? Are you tired of waiting and waiting and waiting for Windows to boot? Are you going bald due to excessive hair-pulling? Do you want to kill your computer? If the answer to any of these questions is either "Yes" or "No" then you're at the right place! This is my comprehensive guide to destroying your computer without leaving any trace. It's about time we hit back.

The Hard-Where Kill: This is a technique that I have perfected over a period of time, and is perhaps the most effective way to destroy a computer. It involves speed, skill and timing, and should be practiced on a watermelon first (avoid pumpkins; they're a cliché). Contrary to a popular fairy tale that says the motherboard is the heart of the computer, I have recently made the startling discovery that computers are, in fact, heartless. This explains their lack of emotion, their oblivious indifference to our pleas of help and their disgusting attitude of throwing up sparks after a wet, sloppy kiss.

So, it's wrong to assume that killing the motherboard will effectively kill your computer. You have to be more thorough.

Stand at a height of exactly 22 feet off the ground, hold out a watermelon in front of you and extend your hands as far as they can go. Close your eyes, let go of the fruit and quickly turn back to avoid the splatter – all in one quick motion. This requires a lot of practice, and it's useful to have at least three melons handy. Once you're sure that you've got the technique perfected, go unhook the computer's monitor and imagine that it's the watermelon. It makes for great reality TV too, so be sure to call AXN or any of those other cheap-thrills TV channels to capture the shards of glass and innards of the monitor flying in all directions.

Once the monitor is dead, pick up the motherboard and dump it in your water tank. A clean kill.

Serves them right, the idiot boxes!

The Soft-Snare Kill: This is a more delicate and time-consuming process that requires a lot of patience. Install Windows Vista and wait.

Windows Vista is an operating system that works on the principle of camouflage and deception. Appearances can be so deceptive – it will make the computer feel all warm and cozy and important, but it'll kill the system from the inside completely and comprehensively, over time. All you have to do is wait and smile an evil smile, showing the same amount of sadism and indifference that the computer had once shown you.

Serves them right, the bastards!

The Why-Rus Kill: Computer viruses are ubiquitous in nature. There are people who have spent their whole lives writing malicious bits of code and dangerous programs (because they didn't have anything better to do and their girlfriends/boyfriends ditched them and their parents didn't love them enough), and there are people who have spent their whole lives trying to protect computers from these viruses (because they didn't have anything better to do and their

[66]

girlfriends/boyfriends ditched them and their parents didn't love them enough).

A little-known method of killing a computer is to open up the motherboard and sneeze on it a million times a day, infecting it with snot, dirt, phlegm and of course, the rhinovirus. Invite your family and friends to join you – make a ritual orgy out of it. Mankind, who's been around for so many millennia, hasn't been able to find a cure for this virus, and there's no way in Hell the bloody computers will. Have you ever seen a computer that has a cold? No, I'm sure you haven't. They cease to exist once they catch the virus. It's perfect!

Serves them right, the dumb machines! Contact me for a free demo!

#23: The Dummy's Guide To Breaking Up

Author's Note: You'll notice, as you read this post and a few others later on in the book, that I refer to myself as The Love Guru. *This is a title that I awarded myself. I thought it'd be cool and people would take my fucked-up advice on matters of the heart seriously.*

So, here we are again, after a few rants and a lot more beer, trying to learn some of the basic things in life through the evergreen Dummy's Guide. This time round, I decided to be a bit more human and latched on to topics that are studied and researched the least around the world – breaking up, ditching and getting ditched. Not many people want to talk about it, but psychologically speaking, it's a very easy thing to talk about, especially after a few rounds of vodka. Alcohol loosens tongues.

There are guides to lose a girl and there are guides to lose a guy, but The Dummy's Guide is perhaps the most comprehensive of the lot.

Anyway, I've decided to publish my research here, after careful observations with spy cameras, hidden microphones and tapped telephones. For anyone who is in a relationship they don't want to be in, this is a must read. Follow these techniques and you'll be single again, that's a guarantee. The Love Guru endorses these techniques, by the way, so no need to worry about the credibility of the claims.

It's Not You, It's Me: Popularized by Seinfeld and immortalized by the Love Guru, millions of times, the *It's-not-you-it's-me* routine works wonders when dealing with stubborn partners. I know many of us would just wish that we could say the things we think about, on their faces, but unfortunately, that would get us killed. For instance, there was this girl who once accused me of "taking advantage" of her, and I really wanted to say, "Why don't you go to the mall? I've heard they're giving away lives for free. Get one, bitch," but I ended up saying, "Of course not, baby. You can trust me," and we cuddled the whole night. I broke up with her the next evening using the *It's-not-you-it's-me* routine.

This is what you need to do. Take your partner to a very nice restaurant, sit across the table and look into their eyes and tell them, "Look, this really is not what I had in mind when I started seeing you. I am really crazy in my head and my notions of love and relationships are obsolete. You're a great person and I am sure you deserve someone much better than me."

Then your partner will look shocked, maybe shed a few tears and ask you, "Please don't say such things."

And you should say, "It's not you, it's me. It's just me. I am not the right person for you. Let's not argue further." Hold your partner's hands while saying the line, it adds to the effect. Trust me, this always works.

I Need A Break: This technique is ideal for people below twenty-five years of age, and those who are not ready for a commitment with their partners. More often than not, your partner will be seriously considering marrying you and they would have already named the first three of your unborn kids. So, once you see the signs (excessive drooling around you, stupid look in their eyes, blindly agreeing to whatever you say, every conversation leading to marriage and future and babies), you should make sure that you break it off.

Take your partner to the place where you first went out for a date, or any other nice coffee shop. Tell your partner that you need a break and that you just want to be friends and that you have a career to think about at that moment in your life. Your partner will be confused and won't understand what you're hinting at. Then you should say, "I don't want to date you anymore."

If your partner still doesn't get it, then you shouldn't be with that person in the first place!

[69]

I'm Already Married: If neither of the two routines are applicable to you, then the best and (sometimes) the safest way is to tell your partner that you're already married. Choose a public place to tell them this, because there are chances that they might get violent. To be safe, call the cops beforehand.

The Other Routines: Other guides would probably harp on other routines and the most popular one I found for men was to tell your partner that you're gay. This is a big No-No! Do not tell your partner that you're gay, because you have no idea what effect this will have on your image in the market. Your partner will stop at nothing to make the whole world know that you're gay and that will seriously affect your chances of scoring with anyone else. You can tell them you're gay if you are bisexual and don't mind a few advances from idiots of the same sex.

If you are a woman and you tell your partner that you're gay in the hopes of driving him away, you are in for a rude shock. You can hear the man's heart go "fucking-threesome-fucking-threesome."

If You Get Dumped: Don't worry. Just contact me and tell me your problems and why you were dumped and I will take up your case and figure out a way to make your life better.

#24: The Dummy's Guide To Pissing People Off

Of course! It has to be true! Damn right! You need to piss people off all the time! It's much like the song 'Iris' by Goo Goo Dolls, where he croons, *"...yeah you bleed just to know you're alive!"* We need to irritate people around us all the time to feel alive. What's the point of living if you don't piss someone off, huh? Tell me!

Pissing people off – the heart and soul of our existence. We wouldn't be here doing what we are doing if someone a hundred thousand years ago hadn't pissed someone off and started a war. We wouldn't be here if someone hadn't pissed on someone else's joy! You wouldn't be reading this if someone hadn't pissed me off and made me write this. So, you have to agree with me that it's quite important to piss people off all the time. It's our God-given right. It's why we were given a voice. It's the reason we were given the ability to ridicule and irritate and point fingers and laugh. It's our duty!

So, how do we do it? How do we achieve the perfect balance between pissing someone off and not getting slapped, shot, kicked in the nuts, stabbed in the back, kicked in the nuts, slapped, slapped, punched in the face, kicked in the nuts again and pushed off a cliff? It takes great care and patience to achieve this feat, and it's not easy. You need to pay attention.

Pissing Men Off: Quite easy – take a dig at their manhood. Tell them they're virgins or that their dick is too small and even if they are or it is, they'll vehemently deny it. Watching their face go from a normal beige to various shades of red, blue and orange is quite fun. Men are strange in this issue – I don't know why but they always overplay their sexual exploits and they always add a few inches when asked, and this is the best way to piss them off.

Of course, the only other things that matter to a guy are beer and sports. Ridicule his favorite beer and you might end up on the wrong end of a well-reasoned argument in the middle of the street at midnight until the cops break you up. Ridicule the guy and call him a sissy for watching cricket or golf or baseball, and he'll go stark-raving mad.

Pissing Women Off: Given that sex, booze and sports are the only three things that can effectively piss a man off, you'll find it hard to piss a woman off with these three topics. Women are usually very secure about their sexuality/sex lives and taking a dig at their alcoholic tastes will be like throwing grains of sand at a hurtling train hoping to derail it. And women and sports, well, let's just say that's a door best left unopened. (My Mum thought F1 cars were unmanned battery-controlled toys.)

So, how do we piss off a woman? Easy – take a dig at her age. It always works, no exceptions. Tell her, "Oh, you look so much younger in your photographs!" and she'll hate you with a vehemence second only to a supernova.

Horizontal attacks are also effective. "You seem to have gained some weight," "Is that an extra-large top?" and "How many months due are you?" are the three most effective way to piss a woman off about her weight. Never fails.

But I am duty bound to warn you – Hell hath no fury like a woman scorned. Be careful.

Go ahead! Piss someone off today! Live a little!

PS: I always wanted to write a postscript with a totally useless sentence, just to make you read it and piss you off.

#25: The Dummy's Guide To Long Distance Relationships

"Wait a minute! What is this? The Dummy's Guide? Oh my god, it's back! It's back!" screamed one hysterical groupie who ran into me on the street this afternoon. I didn't know whether to be embarrassed or delighted. In the end, I just managed to nod my head, smile, make appropriate noises, and escape to the safety of my office.

After what seems like a really long time, I am proud to present the rebirth of the Dummy's Guide series – the self-help guides that guarantee results. For the uninitiated, check out the other guides above.

This time, I write about a topic in which I have done very extensive research – women and relationships. I don't claim to know all the answers, of course, but I know just about enough to help all those poor souls who are unlucky enough to be trapped in a long-distance relationship. I have an ulterior motive in writing this post, obviously.

I too, am stuck in a long-distance relationship with a wonderful woman who amazes me with her sudden bouts of weirdness. After a *deja vu* morning that saw me re-live my "gory days" of 2006, when I was rapidly losing my mind and my hair over a dead-end long-distance relationship, I decided to write this guide to help ease the pain and mental agony that many of my fellow men face in similar situations.

Given below are a list of the top five accusations that an unhinged girlfriend/wife/partner can make against you in a long-distance relationship, and the appropriate responses that you can use as rebuttals. These responses are guaranteed to ensure a long-lasting feeling of warmth and love in the unhinged girl's mind, while totally absolving you of any grief, guilt or need. Here goes.

You Never Have The Time To Talk To Me: I'm sorry, I've been too busy talking to other people about you. I've been so held up that I haven't really had time for anything else. Everyone around me seems to want to know about you, and I've told the story of how we met and fell in love a million times in the past three days! (*For added effect:* Each time, with a smile on my face.)

You Don't Communicate Enough! I Don't Know What's Happening In Your Life: If I don't communicate enough, it's probably because there isn't anything interesting to report. In the past few months, the only interesting thing that has happened to me is YOU. There is nothing else happening with me. Without you around, I lead a very boring life.

You Are Never There When I Need You The Most: *The obvious thing to say would be, "Well, neither are you, bitch!" but please refrain from doing so. Instead, say this:* I know I've been preoccupied with certain things of late, but you're always a priority, darling. I will make sure that I'll take the effort to be there for you whenever you need me. You're never off my mind.

I Don't Know Whether This Will Work Out Or Not: Neither did the Shah of Persia, when he set out to walk around the world alone. But he did. He accomplished the seemingly impossible task by sheer faith. Have faith in us, and we will survive. (*PS: There was no Shah of Persia, but she need not know that. Forrest Gump is also a good name to use.*)

My Friend Saw You With Another Woman On The Bike / Car / Mall / Beach: It's true, I won't deny it. I met a friend from school / college and we went out for a coffee / lunch. She called me a hopeless romantic because all I could talk about was you.

For more information on specific scenarios, feel free to contact me. If I'm alive at the end of the day, I'll respond to your mails. If not, then it's been sweet knowing you.

#26: The Party Animal

Author's Note: This was written almost ten years ago, when I was living in Buffalo, NY on a student budget. Oh, I remember those glorious winters when I had to walk in waist-deep snow. I used to wear five layers of clothes under my thick coat and did not take a bath for two weeks straight. I didn't have the money to eat but I always managed to find a few dollar bills lying around for cigarettes.

I've been known to be a party animal ever since I danced butt-naked on the streets of Bangalore. I was three years old then, and I've got no regrets (except for the hiding I got from my Mum later). I'm considered to be the heart and soul of any party I go to – getting drunk and making jokes about myself and laughing along, having a great time and not remembering a damn thing afterwards. But that animal is now on the endangered species list, more out of necessity than a fading desire to be a drunk amnesiac.

Recently, I was invited to a *get-together* – whatever that means – of all the people in my class. Apparently a few seniors were coming too. So, here I was, thinking that this was going to be a great time to get to know these poor sods with whom I have had the misfortune of spending the last six months with. I thought I'd rather like them for what they were not. Wishfully thinking thus, I hailed a cab and got in, carrying my box of precious *Bisi Bele Bath* – a deliciously South-Indian dish that I was going to inflict upon the party. The city was experiencing the worst snowstorm in decades that night and cabs had a two-hour waiting period. The roads were buried knee-deep in snow and I had to struggle to maintain my balance as I climbed into the relative warmth of the cab. There was an old Indian guy behind the wheel and he started lecturing me about personal hygiene all through the journey. I should've seen the ominous signs.

The "party" consisted of twelve-thirteen people with little or no dress sense and we were all cooped up in a tiny room, half of which was taken up by my generous girth. We all sat around in a circle on the carpet — the furniture was nonexistent — and stared at each other with a glass of Sprite in our hands, passing around a huge bowl of potato chips. We smiled occasionally, more out of unsaid pity than anything else, and waited for our tummies to growl. The others had prepared some or the other dish and I was waiting to get my hands on them.

The moment the conversation — whatever little there was of it — turned to familiar grounds like Bollywood, the weather and food, I excused myself and went out into the corridor, where I called up my friend Vatson and begged her to help me. She failed to help me come up with an excuse to run out of the place. She apologized, and before hanging up, she suggested that I call for a cab soon, because the two-hour wait had gone up to three hours, courtesy of some fresh snow.

I was going to be stuck in that place for three more hours! I was running out of options and sanity and at that time, jumping out the window would not have been such a bad idea after all.

"Hey, great party, isn't it?" said some asshole.

"Yeah man," agreed another.

They sipped their drinks and kept quiet for the next twenty minutes. I almost tore my hair out. There was no music system, else I'd have drowned my sorrows in some beautiful Metallica symphony.

Finally, it was time to eat, and I've got to agree, the food was good. I hogged down whatever I could lay my hands on and announced that my cab was on its way. By the looks on their faces, I knew half the room wanted to kiss me. Then I broke the bad news to them. There was only going to be one cab and it could hold only 6 people. The others had to wait for it to drop the first batch and return to pick them up. This time, no one wanted to kiss me.

With ten minutes for the cab to arrive, I picked up my coat, laced up my boots and went out the door, wishing everyone a good night. Someone suggested I stay there overnight and "have fun". If only I had a good sized stone. I politely refused. I said I needed five more people. One girl literally ran out clutching her shoes in her hand. Six of us went down and waited in the cold for the cab to show up.

I put my name on the endangered species list that night.

#27: Oh, The Horror!

Ever seen a horror movie? Ever had that feeling that the obligatory dumb girl in the movie deserved to die? Better still, ever had that cold crawl up your spine just as the door to a dark room is being slowly opened and the haunting music builds up to a loud crescendo and ends in a bloodbath? Well, I'm sure you have. But these things aren't much fun when the movie pauses every five minutes to buffer.

And it's especially not fun when you're cooped up in a room full of giggling girls, who laugh at the dumb heroine's plight or the poor hero's agony or the terrifying evil spirit's helplessness at being trapped inside the screen.

Don't get me wrong – I enjoyed it. I loved every buffering second of it – the frequent trips to the bathroom, the Pepsi, the cookies, the jokes and the realization that the next day was a holiday and we could all wake up at our own sweet times without the courtesy of an alarm clock. But I have this disease that contorts my face into a semblance of a bored expression bordering on the suicidal when I'm really engrossed in a movie, and my friends mistook this to be a homicidal one. My apologies. I'm setting the record straight.

The Exorcism of Emily Rose was a good movie and even though most of us had already watched it thrice, I'd never experienced a horror movie in this manner before, and surprisingly enough, my instinct to stay alive forced me to sleep with a light on.

Take my friendly suggestion – if you want to watch a horror movie with a gang of girls who are susceptible to giggling fits, please keep these three rules in mind before you begin:

1. Make bloody sure that the movie is buffered. DVDs are a safer option for rich kids.

2. Have lots of non-alcoholic drinks at hand. You don't want these girls to get drunk halfway through the movie – it's going to be a disaster.

3. Use a pair of headphones to block out the incessant giggles.

Author's Note: Obviously, this was written at a time when I was so poor that I considered DVDs expensive and I hadn't discovered the joys of piracy yet.

#28: Cursed! Again and Again

...and again! I don't know which side of the bed I woke up on yesterday, but I'm never going to do it again, hopefully. My day wasn't all that bad, as a whole, but for some reason, I got cursed seven times. Seven different people in seven different situations cursed me with unspeakable pejoratives.

Here're the situations, as best as I can remember them, and I'll let you decide whether I deserved all the colorful language that was hurled at me.

Late afternoon, I was riding my bike in heavy traffic and singing a romantic song, thinking of my girlfriend, and gleefully unaware of the honking and road rage all around me, when all of a sudden, a lunatic *auto rickshaw* (or a *tuk-tuk* to those who are familiar with the phrase) careened out of the corner and scraped my front fender. I'm not a person who loses his temper easily, and as long as I'm not hurt or my wallet is not hurt, I don't care. So, I just whipped out my middle finger at the auto driver and continued my singing. This guy, I don't know why, popped his head out the vehicle and screamed, "*Ninakkan!*" and drove off. This word, in my language, has something to do with elder sisters and incest. I don't have an elder sister, but still, I was kind of annoyed. I hadn't raised my voice, only my finger, and I don't think I deserved this insult.

The second incident occurred when I was walking down the road from my office, with a breath mint in my mouth. I was rolling the piece of mint with my tongue, when I passed a mother and her small girl, walking past me. Just then, my tongue made a smacking sort of a noise because of the piece of candy, which the mother mistook for something else. She turned around and glared at me and *called me a pervert*. I knew there was no point trying to reconcile. I just shrugged and moved on.

The next three instances happened almost simultaneously. I was in my friend's place in the evening, watching a cricket match and munching on some peanuts, when three of my other friends walked in. They said the following things to me:

Friend 1: *"Hey asshole! How's it hanging?"*

Friend 2: *"You bastard! How're you man!?"*

Friend 3: *"Fucking moron! Long time no see!!"*

Just when I was about to sigh and resign to my fate of being cursed all day long, there was an ad running on TV, which screamed out, *"Nikhil's a loser!"* I mean, why couldn't the ad feature some other name? If they wanted to portray a loser, then why choose a winning name like Nikhil?

Lastly, when I realized that my day had been extremely weird and that I'd been cursed enough number of times, things just got worse. While riding back home from my friend's place, late at night, I was whistling to myself, when I stopped at a red light. I was still whistling, when I heard a scream of anger next to me. There was a couple on a bike – the man riding and the woman sitting behind him – glaring at me, the guy about to take his helmet off. He said, *"Loafer! Stop eying my girl!"*

I lost my temper a bit. Just a bit. I was about to open my mouth to retort when the lights changed and the guy flipped a finger at me and rode off at full speed.

I started thinking on my way back, that maybe it's not a good idea to sing or whistle when riding a bike. Maybe it's something else altogether. I don't know. I've been wronged and I demand justice!

#29: Cash Back!

There's one in every family.

I'm sure most of you have had this experience before. There's this freaky guy whom I have had the misfortune of being friends with. According to him, we're the "best-*est* of friends" and according to me, he's an unwanted piece of garbage who just doesn't know when he's not needed and just doesn't understand the fact that he's a burden on this earth. I pity him. If you look at his face, the word *dumb* pops in your mind. His body fat is unevenly distributed, his eyes are lop-sided, his brain is in the wrong place, and he would be automatically entered into the Special Olympics if he went anywhere near the venue. If he wasn't dropped on his head as a child, I seriously wonder what sort of parenting he had to go through to turn out as he has.

I may be a bit too harsh on him, but that's the way he is. I can't help it. Would you believe that I'm actually down-playing this mentally-challenged embarrassment to nature who thinks I am his friend?

Anyway, I had lent this guy two hundred rupees, a small amount considering the amount of money I make. This was over a month ago. He promptly forgot about it until I gently reminded him that he owes me. He immediately made out a check for two hundred rupees and gave it to me. Now, this was the first time I was handling a check for so less an amount and I was like, "Dude, it's just two hundred! You can give me the cash when you have it. No hurry, I was just reminding you in case you forget."

So, he said, "No man, take it. I don't want to keep you waiting." I was surprised but hey, money's money. So, I took the check and deposited it in my bank the next day. A week later, the check bounced.

The bank charged me a penalty of 25 rupees for the bad check and I was mad with rage. I called up the dumb freak and told him that his check had bounced and that he now owes me 225 rupees, for which he asked me, "What do you mean the check bounced?"

"There was no money in your account, you moron. The check bounced," I said.

"Oh, ok," he said and told me to come near an abandoned building off the highway to collect the money. I was a bit scared and was wondering if he was going to kill me in that secluded place and make it look like an accident or something. I had no idea how his under-developed mind worked. He finally showed up after making me wait an hour and handed the money over to me. I asked him why he called me so far away from civilization. Instead of replying, he smiled and put his hand inside his shirt pocket and I freaked out a bit. He was going to shoot me dead, I knew it! I was about to shout bloody murder, when he took out a cigarette and said, "For smoking, man! My folks don't know I smoke so I usually go far away from home to light up."

I smoked one cigarette with the demented freak and went home, where my Mum told me that she had gone to a wedding that day and that the demented guy's family is related to us in a distant way.

As I said, there's one in every family, where the process of evolution stops for good.

The Art Of Writing Letters

Author's Note: I'm the ultimate hypocrite, I think. I give a lot of advice to people on how to fall in love, what to do once you fall in love and how to get out of it. But when it comes to myself, I curse Cupid each time a relationship doesn't work out. Actually yeah, fuck him. It's all his fault.

#30: Letter To Cupid

Dear Cupid,

When you first met me, you chose a lovely, red, pointy arrow and shot it right through my heart. I bled and bled but you didn't really care. You moved on to your next victim, impaling everyone you met. I so hate you for pulling that arrow out forcefully and hurting me more. When you did that to me, you not only ensured that two lives would never be the same again, but you also made sure that I can never be affected by your childish charms and sharp arrows again.

Just because you're a child with wings and you carry around a bow and arrow, you think you can play around with people's lives and emotions and feelings? Who gave you that right, you idiot child? Just because you are written about in books and sung about in stupid love songs, you think that you are the ultimate puppet master, making your victims dance to your tunes? You're nothing but a spoiled brat. Your curly, blonde hair, your red and rosy cheeks and those brilliant blue, innocent eyes may fool others but not me.

I think I know what you're planning for me.

You want me to take the tried and tested path of begging for your arrow to be impaled again in my heart, drinking myself silly in filthy places and in my stupor, calling out for that cardiac pain again and stabbing myself with chemicals in the hope of seeing your bright wings again – well, think again, asshole! I am not going to give you that pleasure. I am well and truly in control of my emotions and for all I care, you can take those arrows of yours and thrust it up your ass. I don't really care how you do it, but given a chance, I'd do it myself. I dare you to come before me again, as you did last time. Stand before me like a man and face me.

Oh, I forgot – you're a child.

So, here's what I really had to say to you, Cupid: drop dead!

Sincerely,
Me

#31: Letter To Cupid, 2012

Dear Asshole,

Here we are again, in 2012. I'm still here, single as fuck, and you're still there, dancing around with your gay wings and your gay arrows. I wrote to you earlier, about four years ago and you promised me that the next time would be different. You are a filthy liar and nothing more. If I look back on this year, all you've given me is hope, despair and embarrassment. What the hell is the matter with you? Can't you do your job right?

So, in light of all that you've done for me this year and everything you've done for me in the past, I raise both my big fat middle fingers to you. Go suck an orange, kid.

Do you remember how I signed off my last letter to you? You don't? Drop dead.

In all sincerity,
Go Fuck Yourself.

#32: Letter To An Asshole

Dear Asshole,

It's been nice knowing you for so long. Really, when you stumbled upon my blog a month ago, I never realized we would be forging such a strong bond of indifference. With all that's been happening in my life right now – work tensions, women, money issues, women, health issues, women, etc – I really think that I can do without your incessant stupidity.

You remind me of a stupid monkey-like creature that has been dead for a million years; it died because it mistook professional courtesy for unconditional love. Of course, since I haven't even met you, I don't know whether you actually *look* like the stupid monkey-like creature, but I'd put my money on it.

You are sexually insecure and your parents hate you. You were a mistake to begin with. You were the result of one night's heavy drinking nine months before you were born. Your parents are ashamed of you. That's why they named you like that. You are ashamed of your lineage, and you can't do anything about it, except roam around the internet harassing people when you could do something useful and kill yourself.

All said and done, my dear asshole, I still like you. I like you a lot, because the world needs people like you. Where else will the scientific community get human specimens for experimental trials? Where else will car manufacturers get dummies for their crash tests? The world would have been a boring place without you, my friend.

My dear asshole, I salute you with a lot of feeling, and I am sorry that you can't see which finger I'm holding up. Go rot in hell.

Sincerely,
Me

Disclaimer: Asshole is real. He is an asshole. He is an ancient monkey-like creature. Maybe someday, when he kills himself, I'll throw a grand party where I'll reveal his name, till then, let's play the guessing game.

#33: Jingles, Jangles & Balls

Dear Santa,

How've you been? I hope you're keeping yourself warm? Guess what: It's that time of the year again, where we all become spies and secret agents. The Secret Santa game started in office today, and each one of us picked names. It's all hush-hush, with everyone guessing and double-guessing who their Secret Santa is.

I've been trying to reach you for the past two days, but you're not answering your phone.

I've been a good boy this year, Santa. I really have. You have to believe me. I did my chores, I've remained single, I've forgiven them all, I've forgotten them all, I've been honest (to an extent), I've been regular on the blogs, I've given up trying to quit smoking, I've not used more than a hundred swear words a day, I've not broken many hearts, I've not given the finger to too many losers, I've prayed hard for beer, I've worked hard, I've partied harder, I've hardly touched anything that I'm not supposed to touch, I've written no more than two hate mails a week, I've haven't killed anyone or anything, I've done all that I could to maintain my level of atrociousness, I've washed myself before and after, I've been clean (in a non-drug-related way; you know what I mean. Wink), I've not been wasting my food, I've fed a few hungry people, I've been nicer to dogs this year, I've done my bit for the environment, I've stayed out of jail, I've donated blood and other bodily fluids to people in need, I've thought really hard about running a marathon, I've not made prank calls, I've not asked for much from you before, and we both know that you've not given anything I've asked for, you jackass.

But this time, please, there's something I really want and I really hope that you're reading this: please grant me my paycheck. That's all I ask.

Love,
Nikhil

#34: Your Missing Comment

Dear Mystery Girl,

I don't know if you remember the first time we interacted. It was, like so many other hapless souls do these days, over the internet. You commented on a post of mine and then accused me of deleting it. What started out as a friendly exchange of emails soon turned into a deeply meaningful conversation in which hopes and fears were shared.

We had not seen each other and we were already beginning to feel like we have known each other for a very long time.

Then we met. We fell in love but we were unable to express it. You were unsure and I was still a kid. We made promises to keep in touch and drifted apart.

But the universe had other plans for us. We found each other again in professional avatars and we both tried to ignore the white elephant in the room that always loomed over us. Those un-kept promises and those unsaid words of love and passion. We worked well together and achieved little, but it was always a pleasure to be around you. I haven't met anyone else with whom I have shared so much. You know my deepest fears and my darkest moments. You are aware of things and people that depress me and you have helped me through my darkness.

We drifted apart when you mysteriously disappeared from my life. When I found you again, you said, "The people who want you in their lives will find you." That made me smile.

We've laughed, fought, almost cried, smoked, smoked up and gotten drunk together. We've read, written and composed for each other. We've cursed each other and we've praised each other. And even though we're on different continents and separated by mountains, volcanoes and oceans we've sailed through it all.

Mystery Girl, you are a great friend, a fantastic woman and will always be the one that got away. I wonder what would have happened if we'd hooked up and given it a whirl. Oh well, if wishes were horses, I'd have a stable by now.

Yours always,
Me

#35: Who Ate My Onions?

Author's Note: India has this unique disease in which, at least once a year, onion prices skyrocket. People have resorted to stocking up on onions before this happens. Yeah, we are warned about a month in advance about the price hike. Strange.

With the onion prices in India touching the lower levels of the stratosphere and threatening to break the planet's escape velocity, it's only fair that people resort to innovative methods of making and saving money. This will follow the typical Darwinian principle of strong-eat-weak and rich-screw-over-poor. Come to think of it, I think Darwin deserves a Nobel Prize in economics – I'm sure a lot of people think that his *Origin of Species* was a metaphorical work describing the economic recession.

I went to the supermarket last evening to pick up some vegetables for the empty fridge, and after spending some time near the onion counter contemplating the steeply rising prices, my attention was diverted to two people who were fighting nearby.

Here's how the conversation went, roughly:

Fat Guy With Ponytail: What did you call me?

Thin Guy With Ribs Sticking Out: Nothing, sir. I did not say anything.

FGWP: No, you called me fat!

TGWRSO: No, No! I did not!

FGWP: Admit it. You were stealing onions from my basket and then, when I caught you, you called me fat!

TGWRSO: Sir, you got me wrong. I was not stealing. I was just looking at them. Please sir, I am not a thief!

FGWP: Likely story! You should be flogged!

At this point, the thin guy with ribs sticking out started pleading pathetically with folded arms in a typically Indian manner. This brought the store manager rushing towards the commotion.

Store Manager: What is happening here? What's the racket about? Stop fighting, sir (addressing the Fat Guy).

FGWP: Good you came! Are you the manager?

SM: Yes sir! I am. What is the problem here?

FGWP: This guy was stealing my onions! Trash him!

SM: (Looking at the thin guy and then back to the Fat Guy) Sir, he was not stealing your onions.

FGWP: What?? I tell you, this guy was stealing! Are you calling me a liar? I saw him reach out and pick up two onions from my basket while I was looking away!

SM: Sir, that's not possible. This fellow works here at the store. He is in charge of the onion section.

The fat guy was somewhat caught off guard, but he held his position and continued his tirade.

FGWP: You hire thieves in your store! Do you know how much these onions cost? An arm and a leg! He was stealing it!

SM: Sir, give him a chance to explain. (Turning now to the thin guy) Rama, explain yourself. Did you pick up two onions from this man's basket?

TGWRSO: Yes sir. But –

FGWP: Aha!

TGWRSO: ...but I wasn't stealing!

SM: Then why did you pick them up?

TGWRSO: They dropped into his basket by mistake. These onions belong to this man here.

And he pointed at me.

I looked into my own basket, and true enough, I was two onions short. The fat guy looked at me, then at the thin guy, then at the store manager and then back at me, trying to figure out how I fit into his whole onion-thievery theory. Apparently, I didn't. He just handed me back my onions and muttered, "Sorry" under his breath to all three of us and walked away.

#36: My Pervert Uncles

There's one in every family. There are two in mine.

The first one is a seventy-year-old pervert. He's my uncle on my Dad's side of the family and has always had the ugly habit of addressing small (male) kids as, "Hi Miss!" and "How are you, Miss?" Loudly. In public.

If that isn't uncomfortable enough, he still follows the ritual. I ran into him at a cousin's wedding recently, and even though I'm taller and bigger than him, he smiled at me through his dilapidated, yellow teeth and said, "Hello, Miss!"

I cringed and moved away, oblivious to his hurt sentiment. A minute later, I heard him say the exact same thing to my brother, who is taller and bigger than me. I caught my brother's eye and we both ignored the old pervert and moved away. This guy has kids of his own, who are both grown men and I feel sorry for the fact that they have to endure this kind of sexually explicit torture each day. I won't be surprised if those two kids grew up feeling very confused about their sexuality. I think it borders on sexual harassment.

The second pervert in my family is another seventy-year-old uncle on my Mum's side, who just can't stop touching himself in "special" places in front of everyone. I had the misfortune of running into him as well during the wedding, and while he shook my hand, he twirled his other hand inside his white *lungi*. I rushed to the restroom and washed my hands with soap vigorously. Who knows where that hand of his has been?

As I stepped out of the restroom, my brother ran past me and starting washing his hand.

[98]

#37: Gokarna & Why I Go There

This one goes out to all those unfortunate, uninitiated and uninspired individuals. Get off your high horses and read this.

There may be a hundred reasons why a person goes to Gokarna. People wanting to get laid, people wanting to score weed and get high, people looking for a nice, secluded beach and people wanting to offer their prayers in one of India's most sacred temples. I don't know if there are any other reasons, and frankly, I don't really care why people go there.

I go there for a totally different reason, and it's none of the above.

I lead a difficult life. I need to balance my passion to work, my unceasing urge to travel and roam aimlessly across the country, my singularly fierce attraction to beaches and my diminishing bank account. Juggling these four volatile substances while playing air hockey with the family, the bosses, the peers, the juniors, the friends, the foes, the creditors, the goons, the loons, the whackadoodles, the geniuses, the crap, the stench and the slippery slopes of bankruptcy, unemployment and loneliness around every corner is taking its toll on my nerves.

There are very few things I'm passionate about, and those that I am passionate about, I am so with a vehemence unseen in anyone else, for anything else. I do not go to Gokarna to "do drugs." I do not go to Gokarna to "sleep with women." I do not go to Gokarna to "drink drinks." I do not go to Gokarna to visit the temple and offer my prayers. I do not go to Gokarna for the sea food. I do not go to Gokarna for the rustic beauty of the village. I do not go to Gokarna to ogle at half-naked women lounging in the sun. I do not go to Gokarna because I love beaches and water. I do not go to Gokarna to swim in the ocean. I do not go to Gokarna to live. I do not go to Gokarna to die.

I go to Gokarna once every three months because I need to get away from the typical Indian tragedy that my life is fast unraveling to be; to clear my head of all thoughts – good and bad; to reboot myself. I go to Gokarna because it's the only place on Earth that welcomes me without judging who I am or what I have done. I go to Gokarna because that is the only place on Earth where I am at peace. Completely.

I have a rock out in the sea, which I call my own, at Om Beach. It's a bit of a hike to get to the top of the rock, and once I do, I sit looking out at the waves crashing into me on all sides, rising twenty feet high and spraying me with a mist of cold, salty seawater. I listen to the rush, the gurgle, the power and the wordless songs of the waves, and as I stare out into the horizon, imagining a place beyond comprehension, where the sky kisses the ocean, I realize that I am peaceful, within and without.

Nothing of what is happening in my life matters here. Time stands still for me, for the forty-eight hours I'm here. I put my feet up at a café, sipping sweet tea and reading a good book, or people-watching on the burning, golden sands. I take a nice pleasant walk up to Kudle Beach through thick brambles and open moors and I wade in the white sands until the sun starts to set. I walk back amidst the gathering darkness to Om Beach, walk all the way up to Half Moon and back again. As night descends around me, so does the peace, deeper inside me.

I need this. I can't do without it. For the unfortunate, uninitiated and uninspired individuals, I recommend it. The only thing I get high on, when in Gokarna, is Gokarna itself.

#38: Gully Cricket Season

After recent events in the world of cricket, it's that time of the year again, when Sundays are reserved for playing gully cricket!

I have always been a cricketer, starting at the tender age of 12. Now, it's been almost three years since I held a bat in my hand and played the game, and yesterday, it was back to basics! In front of our house, there's a good 20 yards of space to play cricket in, and when we were still young and innocent, kids from the entire neighborhood got together to play. I learnt to play the game here, in front of my house, and yesterday, I walked down memory lane again.

I bought a tennis ball and dusted my old bat and coaxed my terrorist brother to abandon his studies and play with me. We started playing something called "short cricket" where the batsman can get out with a "pitch catch" or by hitting the ball out of the compound. We played for nearly three hours, with a cousin of ours, who stays close by, also joining in.

I had almost forgotten the quirky little things like calling out "Ball, please!" to passersby, whenever the ball went out of the gate and on to the main road; calling out "Fast Appeal!" whenever the ball missed my bat and hit the wicket; refusing to give up my wicket unless there was hard evidence that the ball hit the makeshift outline of the wicket on the wall; running behind the ball trying to prevent it from reaching the other end of the compound for a boundary; and all the other funny little things that kids do when they play cricket.

We reminisced about the time when cricket in our compound was a major event – kids from all over the neighborhood would come to play here – we once had installed a 60-watt bulb through some very ingenious engineering and played through the night – our very own version of floodlight cricket! Oh, those were the days!

We stopped playing when I hit the ball out of the gate and it landed inside a passing auto. The auto guy never realized it and drove away with the ball inside. Bastard!

#39: The Love Guru

Author's Note: This is me, giving advice to men on how to pick up women. This is outdated information, and I strongly urge you not to follow this. If you do, then you're on your own. I hereby absolve myself of all responsibility.

This post is meant primarily for men, and single ones at that.

Men who want to try out their luck in wooing a woman and want some inside information on how to go about doing this without being slapped in public, can read this with the assurance that they won't be disappointed. This post comes from someone who's been there and done that when it comes to asking women out on dates, making a complete fool of himself and finally, succeeding. If women want to read this, please do. It's probably going to make you smile at how little men know about women.

No offense is meant to anyone, unless specifically named.

Ok, first things first, my fellow readers – ask yourself the following three questions and if and only if the answer to all three is "Yes" then continue. Otherwise, this post is not for you. Women, ignore the previous two sentences.

1. *Are you a man?*
2. *Have you ever had a crush before?*
3. *Was your crush a woman?*

Ok, now that we've eliminated the kids and the gay ones, let's get down to a serious information-dissemination session.

Women don't like nerds. Don't show off your intelligence to women. Act dumb. Not too dumb, because that could be a huge turn-off. Show them that you're a perfectly normal, average guy, who flunks a couple of exams and yet manages to get a job in a pretty nice company. And I don't mean a call-center. Call center guys are *not* the 'hot trend' nowadays.

Let's take a hypothetical example, you'll understand better. Suppose there is this really *really* hot chick and you want to ask her out to dinner. The first thing you should do is to drop the idea. She's not in your league and all the hot chicks are already taken. So, look elsewhere.

Suppose there is a fairly hot (and very cute) girl, who's single and whom you're interested in. Now, we're talking! You have a chance to score a romantic dinner here! The formula is very simple – wear a black leather jacket over a very white round-neck tee-shirt and wear blue jeans and brown hiking boots. Don't overdo the bling factor because you'll look like a poor Indian wannabe-rapper. No earrings, no rings on your fingers and most of all, no silver/gold watches that dangle.

Walk really slowly when you're with her and give her ample time to look at you and form her opinion. Even if you're in a hurry, whenever you pass her seat, slow down and walk in ultra-slow-motion. It helps. Do not bank on finding women in your new school or college or your new workplace. Go and hunt them out in all the places you never usually visit. The fact that you don't visit these places and the fact that you're single might give you a clue.

Bald men are considered hot by some women, but before you go shaving off your precious hair, try to get the girl to tell you if she likes bald men. Not all men look good without hair. Some men have an unnatural bulge in their faces, and if you remove your hair, you look like that ugly alien from *Alien*. Big turn-off, don't do it.

The type of watch you wear plays a huge role in whether the girl accepts your offer of dinner or not. I suggest something black, not too flashy and something that doesn't have hearts or bubbles on their faces. The hands of the watch must *not* be Mickey Mouse's gloved hands.

Asking a woman out on a date is quite a tricky situation and can have disastrous consequences. From a simple "No" to spending a night in jail, anything could happen depending on how you ask them out. Some despo-self-help books will tell you that the direct approach is the best way, but take my word for it, it's not! Asking her out has to be a long-drawn arduous process in which, her tastes and dislikes have to be properly researched.

Since this depends on individual women, I won't say much on this, except that you should not go up to the girl and say, "Hi, wanna eat?"

The choice of restaurant is also vital in building a fruitful relationship with the girl. Don't take vegetarian girls to Barbeque Nation or KFC.

Being funny is absolutely vital, but make sure people are laughing at your jokes and not at you. It's easy to get confused. And if they're laughing at you, then laugh with them and call yourself a moron, because some girls like that.

Be charming, be witty and be dumb. I know you're probably very confused by now, but I can tell you that once you read this post again, you'll feel really confident on approaching that girl of your dreams. Just don't make it a nightmare for her.

May the force be with you!

#40: XP? Vista? Sanity?

There've been a lot of people who have advised me against using Windows Vista, but so far I've been giving them a deaf ear. Yesterday, I realized just how truthful their words were.

My desktop computer is an ancient piece of garbage that belongs in the antiques department of a museum, and unwittingly, I decided to load Windows Vista on it, a few months back. It performed quite well, considering its age and capacity. Vista, being graphic-heavy, soon began to eat into my computer's memory and yesterday, the damn thing just refused to boot no matter how much I tried. It gave up and I could almost hear it scream for mercy. Being a kind-hearted guy, I decided to heed and made up my mind to switch back to XP. It was a simple task – remove Vista, install XP, be happy. But, being God's yo-yo has its own perks and I soon found myself in a rut.

I went to friend's place where he gave me a couple of XP installation CDs. I plugged in the first one, and saw that it contained the NFS game. I plugged in second one and saw that it contained the proper XP installation files. I happily booted the system from the CD and formatted the entire C drive, hoping to install XP. Halfway through the installation, I realized that I hadn't written down the product key, which had been scribbled on the disk itself. I prayed, removed the disk and tried to write down the 25-digit product key, when I realized that I would have a long night ahead.

I couldn't read what was written on it.

It had been scribbled so badly that most of the letters (or numbers?) were illegible. I tried different combinations – there was one particular letter that could have been an "H", an "M", an "N" or an "A."

I tried all these combinations, and none of them worked. There were five letters that were doubtful, and the number of combinations of these five letters came up to 45,349 according to my poor math. So, I abandoned the effort and sent my brother out to his friend's place to get another copy of an XP installation disk.

I had to bribe him, but he did it. He came back with a disk that looked all right. When I tried to install XP with this disk (thankfully, the product key was clearly written), the installation crashed halfway, claiming that the disk was corrupt and couldn't be read. I was very close to pulling my hair out when the power went out and I was bathed in darkness.

When the power came back on a couple of hours later, I decided to give the damn thing one last try. I switched on the machine, and immediately got an error message, which said, "Boot Sector Fail. Press Any Key To Continue."

I pressed a key, and the computer shut itself down. It's now a paperweight that looks like a computer.

Listen carefully. Can you hear God laughing at me?

#41: The PR Lingo

Being a public relations man has exposed me to a lot of interesting words and phrases, things that I'd never heard before, and things that caused me considerable distress (being a language purist) when I first heard them. Some of these are:

Sit On This: This is used while referring to an issue that has to be discussed or a crisis that has to be handled or a presentation that has to be finished or a document that has to be written or just about anything that has to be done. "Don't worry, I'll sit on this and finish it!" Sounds more like a chicken-murderer plotting his move rather than a serious professional, but I'll have to adapt.

Revert Back: A grammatically-incorrect connotation of the more popular "Reply back," this phrase generally refers to the process of replying to emails and text messages or even phone calls that have to be returned. When I first heard the sentence, "Nikhil, the client has sent us a time for the meeting. Please revert back to him," I had a sly smile all day long.

Collateral: Completely and absurdly contrary to *all* the accepted definitions of the word, "Collateral" in PR lingo, refers to any and all documents that the PR firm gives to its clients, including the clients' profiles and companies' backgrounds, media notes, press releases and the kitchen sink. This is quite a strange term to use, because every time I hear, "Nikhil, have you seen the collateral?" my mind thinks of the movie.

Dip Stick: Ahem! All perversions aside, the phrase "Dip Stick" refers to a survey conducted among journalists, to gauge their understanding of current affairs. This happens whenever a new brand is launched or an old brand is being re-marketed or whenever PR folks feel that they haven't spoken to journalists in a while. We call up journalists and ask them, "There's this new company called so-and-so. Have you heard of it?" More often than not, the journalists hang up the phone.

Boiler Plate: I first heard this phrase a few days back, when someone asked me, "Nikhil, where's the boiler plate on this press release??" I looked back blankly and said, "Uh, what the fuck are you talking about?" Apparently, it's spelt "boilerplate" and refers to a brief note about the client that has to be included on all press releases. Weird, indeed. Something of a pot-boiler to spice up a bland release?

So, there it is. There're a few other weird instances where the English language has been massacred, but I think I've sinned enough for one day.

#42: A Man's Best Friend

... is not a dog, to put a common misconception to rest. It is, on the contrary, a very nicely-blended mix of scotch and soda, with lots of ice.

I had been to a cocktail-dinner party last night at a seedy pub in the city, which had seen better days and the food left a lot to be desired. I wasn't dressed appropriately, I had a bad headache, I had no inclination to attend the party, and yet, I had to go to fulfill certain commitments.

So, I was sitting around, watching the horny cameramen take snaps of those vile and vulgar Page 3 crowd, and thought to myself, "Nikhil, you're here, amidst a bevy of apparently hot chicks and over-fed, rich men and you're wearing a dirty white shirt with sweat stains, a pair of trousers that are frayed around every corner and some weirdly horrifying pair of floaters – what're you missing?"

My brain answered promptly: A drink!

I made my way to the crowded bar, where the drinks were on the house, and I got myself a scotch-and-soda, and sat back and enjoyed the fake smiles around me. I watched the facade as a couple of dumb publicity-hounding chicks in short skirts came up to me and said, "Hey, you are from - ?"

I looked at them and said, "No, I am Nikhil," and gave them my best I'm-not-interested smile.

They got the message and stopped following me around. Every room I entered in that pub, the terribly omnipresent Page 3 crowd was busy hugging complete strangers and getting their photos clicked. And the photographers from these cheesy tabloids couldn't get enough of them. "Get a room," I wanted to scream out, when I realized that they had.

Anyway, I came back home around midnight from the party, and my only faithful companion throughout the party had been my ever-present glass of scotch-and-soda. And when, on my way back through the hauntingly empty streets of the city at midnight, a pair of dogs chased me, barking their lungs out, for almost two kilometers, I decided that a man's best friend is not really a dog. Dogs tend to change loyalties the minute someone offers them a juicier bone.

In a way, street dogs and those Page 3 photographers are similar – one is a filthy cross-breed that lurks the streets searching for a juicy bone and the other is a street dog.

#43: Bay Of Pigs!

Men are pigs.

They say that God created men because he was bored and that He created women because he needed a challenge. Come to think of it, this is rather true. Men are the blueprint while women are the masterpiece. There have been posts and books and speeches and movies about what a woman wants in a man, but none of them match up to the extensive research that I have done on the subject.

There are a variety of different characteristics in a man that a woman looks for, and not all of them are very obvious. Over the past 24 years of my life, I've come across different women with different tastes but there are a few that are common to every woman. Men can consider this post as an eye-opener and take stock of what qualities they lack, and women can consider this post as an easy read and be amazed at my insight into the female mind.

Sense of humor: Most women look for funny men, and this is where I am serious competition to most of you guys out there. But be warned, being funny does not mean cracking lame jokes and making complete idiots of yourself. It's the wit that counts and not your ability to remember jokes. Every situation can be turned around to your advantage while talking to women, and you need to make sure that you don't overdo the funny-guy act. I've preached about this before, and I say it again – make sure you're laughing with them, and recognize when they're laughing at you!

Build: Women are very realistic, unlike men, and they know that not all men can have a body like Schwarzenegger or look like Pitt. Women do not always look for a well-built, muscular body in a man. You may be a flabby piece of shapeless dough or you could be stick-thin, it doesn't matter to most women as long as you can live up to the other requirements. Of course, having a sexy body comes as an added advantage. This is where we men need to learn, and stop looking for Jenna Jameson's boobs in every woman we meet. We need to be realistic, and not stupidly optimistic. All women are hot, no exceptions.

Chivalry: The concept of chivalry, for most men, stops at holding the door open to women. Wake up, men! That's not all what women look for in the chivalry department. While walking with a woman on the road, you need to let her walk on the safer side, thus ensuring that you protect her from the splash of water when a vehicle zooms by and also to protect her from the occasional hit-and-run, by taking the hit yourself. Chivalry can also be very subtly displayed by defending her arguments, even if you don't believe in them, while in a group. This doesn't mean that you become a sneaky yes-man. It takes great skill and greater patience to hold your own and also defend her while arguing in a group. Women like that in a man, someone who can argue with confidence and the moment you start backing her arguments, you become her ally.

Possessiveness: Women like men to be possessive about them. It makes them feel special and wanted. Don't overdo this, because then you would look like a psycho stalker. Tell her at every opportunity that you're there for her and that you'd go out of your way to help her out and make her feel that you're an irreplaceable part of her daily routine. Again, it takes great skill to achieve this, and for more advice on this, mail me.

Music: Women hate tone-deaf men. Every woman has a particular taste in music and it may not always match yours. Don't rubbish her taste in music. Instead, tell her that your taste in music is childish and that you were just about to change your playlists to match hers. Listen to her favorite tracks with her, and encourage her to play it again if she wants to. You can pull your hair out later, when you're alone.

Sex: Do not, I repeat, do not push the woman for a physical relationship. Women are very, very careful in this matter and if you

[113]

push the wrong buttons (no puns intended) you come across as being sexually frustrated. Be careful.

Family Values: Most women like men who have good family values. Respect her parents and her family and she will like you all the more. Never ever call her dad "Dude!" or "Old Man!" because that will bring down your brownie points.

Fighting: Fights are inevitable in every relationship, and when there are situations where you know that the reason is trivial, just take the blame. Tell her you're sorry and that you won't do such a stupid thing again. No matter how big or small the issue is, the fault always lies with the man. Ingrain this in your mind, because the moment you blame the woman for the fight and the moment you lose your temper a bit, that's the end of the relationship. Remember, you're the loving, caring, chivalrous knight in shining armor. You do not blame the woman. You only do that after you are married.

The Ex- factor: Do not, I repeat, do not maintain contacts with your ex-girlfriends while you're pursuing a woman, or when you're in a relationship. Take my advice on this, the reason she's your ex- is because either one of you did not deserve the other. Women are kind of finicky in this matter, and they take umbrage when you talk to your ex- or even run into your ex- by mistake.

Believe me, what matters most is that you should be authentic in your emotions while dealing with women. A woman is a very clever creature, and there's no such thing as a "dumb" woman. There're only dumb men. They can spot your fake smile and ulterior motives from a mile away.

I am a very strong proponent of long-term, fruitful relationships and that flings are bad for health. So, remember my dear pigs, women want authenticity.

Go ahead. May the force be with you!

#44: Farting Etiquettes

Whatever the size, form or shape, toilet humor has always brought a smile to people's faces. So, even if someone does not like the idea of a whole post on farts, what the fart? I'll still write it.

I have always harbored an admiration for the powerful forces of nature. Wind energy is the next best thing to fossil fuels, and as long as there's food on the planet, there will be farts.

Breaking wind is an essential fart of human nature. The fart of the matter is, no one can hold it any longer than two hours. This has been scientifically proven. By me.

There are certain etiquettes when it comes to unleashing our wind upon the unsuspecting public, and not many people adhere to it.

1. If you're alone, then let it out loudly, smile and say, "Wow, what a fart!"

2. If you are in a meeting with four or more people and you very quietly let one loose, then slowly start pushing your chair away from the person sitting next to you and give him/her a dirty look. Others will follow suit. This technique is called *Farting The Blame*.

3. If you're standing in a crowded bus, then make sure that you start pushing your way through the crowd slowly but steadily, moving towards the door, while farting quietly, so that the

stink is distributed evenly throughout the length of the bus. (Not applicable outside India)

4. If you are with your girlfriend / boyfriend and you can't hold it in any longer, then let it rip. If the other person is truly The One and if you guys are meant to be together, he/she will laugh and follow up with one of their own. If not, well, you probably shouldn't have had Mexican for lunch.

5. If you're with someone who's irritating you and you just want them to go away, then do the sonic-boom.

I sincerely hope this small but comprehensive guide helps people in distress. As usual, contact me for a free demo.

#45: And Then, I Dreamt About Shoelaces

I dream a lot, sometimes while driving, sometimes while sitting through a meeting, sometimes while talking to someone and mostly, when I'm sleeping (thankfully). I have this ability to phase out of a conversation in an instant and start dreaming about something totally unrelated and it usually takes a slap or a hard punch to the shoulder to break my reverie.

I dream about a lot of things – women, alcohol, fame, money, glory, women, phones, happiness, women, books, people, friends, enemies, work, office and women. I sometimes dream about women too, but not always.

Anyway, I digress. The coming of the New Year has been tremendous to my spirits. By spirits, I mean the type that is usually consumed orally. But otherwise too, my state of mind has generally been quite a happy one, with lots of hopes (and dreams) about what the new year is about to dish out. One thing I know for sure is that I'm going to remain God's yo-yo. What strengthened my belief in this was an incident that happened one evening, when I was having a conversation with my friend about the lamest of lame topics – shoelaces.

Yeah, I was actually having an intelligent conversation about shoelaces with a friend of mine over a smoke, and he suggested that it was unfair for a person to spend more than three seconds in fastening a pair of shoes. He wanted to invent a self-tying shoelace or something that would save us time. He had obviously never heard of Velcro.

I gently reminded him that many shoes didn't even have laces nowadays and that even if they did, people don't mind spending a bit more than three seconds tying them. But the guy was adamant. Maybe

[117]

because he had been drinking all day and he wasn't in his senses or maybe because he was just being stupid, I don't know. But he was really adamant about the fact that we need automatic self-tying shoelaces.

So, I ventured a bit and actually started dreaming about the possibility of automating everything in life. It wasn't a very good dream, as I had quite a few pervert thoughts (as you can guess). I started giggling to myself at the thought of a fat guy bending over the pot while an automated hand wiped his ass, when this guy decided to slap me on the head quite hard. It was quite a blow – it made me fall off the parapet and land face down on the ground. It wasn't that high a parapet thankfully but three feet can feel like three hundred when you fall face down, and unexpectedly.

I got a text message from the guy the next morning apologizing for his actions and that he'd assumed that I was laughing at his shoelaces idea. He went on to say that though he still believed the idea was worth a shot, he shouldn't have hit me on the head.

I replied to his message, "Thanks, I needed that."

He obviously failed to see the sarcasm and sent a smiley back. What a start to the year!

#46: The Voyeur Next Door

In a nutshell, the forty-year-old woman next door saw me naked this morning. It all happened so fast that it took a good two hours for it to sink in.

I had my bath, wrapped a towel round my waist and came into my room, switched on the fan, stood under it and whipped the towel open. That was when I heard a scream.

I panicked, fell to the floor for cover and picked up the wet towel and covered my body. I slowly stood up and looked around. The window directly in front of me was open and through it, I could see the terrace of my neighbor's house. Amidst all the clothes that were hung out to dry, I saw the shadow of a woman behind a particularly heavy *sari* that sagged the clothesline. It looked like she was covering her face with her hands. I gulped and looked on, and after a while, she slowly peeped at my window from behind her *sari*. On seeing me staring at her, she let out a giggle and ran back into her house.

I stood there, butt-naked but for the towel, drained of all my decency, and wallowing in the realization that the woman next door was a voyeur. I felt used and abused. I felt as if my manhood was up for sale, auctioned off to all middle-aged voyeuristic women. I felt dirty. I felt weird.

Luckily for me, I don't interact much with the neighbors and I'm rarely at home these days, so I think this incident will pass. I hope it does. Jesus Christ! A man can't even change his clothes in privacy!

#47: Let's Have A Conference Call, Folks!

Singapore. Canada. California. New York. And, to ice the cake, Bangalore. The conference call was scheduled to start at 9:30 in the morning, and at 9:29, I realized that the phone in the corner did not have an international calling facility. I was sitting there, all prepared, my papers spread out in front of me, my pen handy, my head going over the different methods of opening the conversation, saying "Hi" or "Hello" or "Good morning", and then, I sat there listening to the sweet yet hideous female voice telling me that this service wasn't available on the phone.

I wondered what to do. The clock ticked away the seconds of the one minute left for me to sign in to the call. I gulped and took a decision that I knew I'd regret. I flipped open my mobile and punched in the numbers. I prayed hard, hoping the call would end in a few minutes. It didn't. It lasted an hour and fifty minutes.

Conference calls, according to me, are a supreme waste of time. I think more work can be accomplished through an email. The first twenty minutes are obviously spent in introducing all the people on the call. The next thirty-odd minutes go away in outlining the agenda for the call. The remaining hour or so is spent in asking people to speak up, apologizing for loud cell phones, apologizing for the rackets behind their respective backs, and finally, asking everyone present if they had understood the last point. More often than not, there will be at least three jerks who would not have paid attention, and they would ask you to repeat the last point.

The frustrating thing about these conference calls is that you cannot abuse anyone verbally. If the same meeting were held over emails, then before sending each mail, you can let out a wonderful stream of expletives, and feel good about yourself. You can question his/her ability to think straight, his/her man-/womanhood, his/her ridiculous name, and lot of other things. But on a conference call, you have to hold your tongue and treat even the most outrageous of jerks with an amount of respect. It takes so much out of you. You can't even make fun of funny names.

Anyway, I have had too many conference calls till now. I think I've devised a formula to survive each one of them. I call it "Apparent Indifference" – if you give the impression to the other jerks on the call that you're indifferent about the outcome, then they'll fall over themselves to spell out each and every point of concern and make sure that each and every doubt has been answered. This, of course, helps me in making the meeting a success.

Oh, I hate conference calls. Of course, the only advantage the conference call has over board-room meetings is that you can fart loudly and get away with it.

#48: Matrix Relocated

There were two pills – a blue one and a red one.

"Take one," he said, and adjusted his black sunglasses. I couldn't fathom why he was wearing dark sunglasses inside the dimly-lit room. I was sure he couldn't see a thing.

"Er, I'm over here, pal," I said, hiding an amused smile.

He turned towards me and used his free hand to raise his glasses. He stuck them over his forehead, looked at me through his blue contact lenses and said, "Don't keep moving about, dude."

"But I – "

"Don't interrupt me!" he said, interrupting me. "Take a pill."

"Why? What are these pills?" I asked, slightly angered with his tone.

"You are the *Round One*. We've been waiting for you for well over a decade. You will save us from the evil machine creatures that haunt us. One of these pills will enable you to see the truth and help us, and the other will enable you to go back to your boring life and your boring blogs and your boring life. You decide."

"You said that already, man," I said.

"What?"

"My boring life – you said that already."

"Yeah. I know. Now decide!" he said and held out his hand, on which nestled two innocent pills – one red and blue.

"Tell me something first," I said. "Why am I the Round One? Is it because I'm fat? Why can't I be something cooler like the Chosen One?"

"Stop wasting time, Round One! Take a pill and save our lives!" he ordered.

I took the red pill and swallowed it. I waited. Nothing happened. I looked at him. "Now what?" I asked him.

"You bastard," he said softly. "You've decided to go back to your boring life, Round One. You have damned us all."

As I woke up, back in my boring life the next day, I decided to reduce some weight. Round One? WTF!

#49: The World's Best Statement Of Purpose

I must confess that I wrote this for a friend three years ago, after a particularly frustrating year of helping her apply for graduate schools in the US of A. As you can imagine, she hasn't spoken to me since.

STATEMENT OF PURPOSE

"Ignorance is Bliss"

The above statement is true in my case. I have absolutely no knowledge or skill. I don't even know why I am writing this. All I know is that I was forced to study right from my first grade, and after 22 long years, I finished my ten-year-schooling. I've heard that your university is the least respected, and the one with the least academic requirements, and so, here I am, applying to you.

The drive to study Life Sciences was instilled in me at a very young age by one of my uncles, who, during his fourth rape session with me, warned me about the dangers of HIV and AIDS. This left a huge impact on my ten-year-old mind. And all our subsequent rape sessions have been with protection, and I was always eager to know more.

If people call you a jerk ten times, does it actually mean that you're a jerk? I don't think so. Because I've been called a jerk a million times, and I still don't think I am a jerk. The best part of accepting me into your university would be that I will not interfere with the amazing research going on there. I will stay away from all the professors and let them carry on with their great work. I particularly liked the research going on about why the cock crows only in the morning. I have a few theories about this which I would be happy to share with you, for a stipend of course. Knowledge doesn't come free, you see.

Anyway, I am looking forward to working with you people and I hope you will grant me admission. I will be invaluable to the university as a perfect scapegoat. I am great as a partner, especially for the men in the university and they can dip their cookie in my coffee whenever they want. Wink!

Thank you,
A poor, misinformed girl from somewhere.

#50: How To Kill Your Landlord

Author's Note: I hate Delhi. I lived in Delhi for 10 months and I moved houses 7 times. I absolutely hate that fucking city. If you live in Delhi, chances are that I hate you too. Fuck you.

After having a major fight with my conscience last night about whether or not I should move out of the zoo I was living in, I slept fitfully, trying to think of different options to hunt down and kill the rats that were running wild in the house. My first instinct was to get the hell out. But slowly, the realization dawned on me that these Delhi rats were super-advanced than their dumb cousins in Bangalore.

They had evolved from being scavengers to being fine-diners; they hardly touched any of the rat poison pellets I'd left for them around the house. That's when I made the decision to leave them be and focus instead on hunting down and killing my landlord.

My landlord is a stupid ninety-year-old fucker, who thinks he's still young enough to drive a car by himself and lift a huge slab of granite all by himself. In hindsight, I think I should've let him do those things and let nature take its own course. But waiting for the elusive heart-attack takes a lot of patience, more than what I have.

So, I decided to take down two pests with one stone and came up with a brilliant scheme, worthy of a jail sentence just for the thought. Here's how the four-step scheme works:

1. Buy a rabid dog.
2. Get the rabid dog to bite the old fucker.
3. Get the rat to bite the rabid old fucker.

4.   Attend two funerals.

I was so pleased with myself that I went in search of a rabid dog this morning. The hunt is still on. I wonder why I keep having flashes of *Hannibal* in my head. I also realized that this is a great money-making scheme. If any of you want to kill your landlord, then get in touch with me. I charge by the hour.

#51: Dental Plaque And The Sugar Doughnuts

Author's Note: I even hate Delhi's dentists and their receptionists.

I'm sure this has happened to everyone. There no point pretending that I'm the only person in the whole wide world this sort of incident has happened to.

There I was, innocently biting into my (tenth) *gulab jamun* while watching Transformers 2: Revenge of the Fallen on my laptop, when a shooting pain in my teeth forced me to drop the bowl of thick sugar syrup all over my bare legs. Nothing fell on my laptop thankfully, and I spent the rest of the morning cleaning the room and myself. Only later did I realize that my teeth needed a dentist's attention.

So, that evening, I walked over to a nearby clinic and got an appointment for later the same evening. Ignoring the bad sentence construction, I walked in at the appointed hour and sat on a plush couch, reading a copy of the latest Outlook magazine and getting rapidly bored.

I must have dozed off because the receptionist shook me vigorously and told me that the doctor was ready for me. In my groggy state, I yawned and mumbled, "Finally. Thank you," when she slapped me hard. I was stunned. I held my cheek where she'd slapped me and looked up at her angry face. She yelled, "What did you say??"

Now, a normal human being would've asked this before slapping someone, but she was, I guessed correctly, a rare find.

"I said *Finally, thank you*," I told her angrily, still clutching my face.

"Oh!" she said, eyes widened in shock and apology. "I thought you said 'Fuck you'. You mumbled so I couldn't hear properly! I'm sorry! I'm really sorry!"

Leaving her to deal with her guilt, I stormed into the dentist's room, feeling angry, stupid and a bit confused at the exchange. He was sitting in the center of the room on a stool, in front of a horrifying dentist's chair, which had all the evil accouterments one usually associates with murderous, villainous doctors in horror movies – gleaming silver instruments that were sharp enough to rip someone's brains out through their noses. I gulped and stood there.

He saw me clutching my face and said, "Hurts, does it?"

"What?" I said, confused, and realized that I was still holding my face. I quickly put my hand down and said, "No, your receptionist slapped me just now."

He didn't seem surprised. "Third one today," he sighed. "I ought to fire her. Anyway, take a seat, please," he said pointing to the torture chair. I looked strangely at him and sat down, lost for words.

"Okay, let me see," he said. He fixed a stainless steel bracket into my mouth to hold it open and turned on the harsh, overhead light and tinkered around my tongue and teeth with a long, steel thing that looked like a bent toothpick. I could see the bright overhead light and the dentist's masked silhouette as he assessed my dental strength.

"There's some plaque," he said. "I'll get my associate to do something about it," and he walked out, leaving me in the chair, mouth open, with the torture device sticking out of it. I twirled my thumb and waited until a short, stocky woman came in and started poking around in my mouth with a metal device that hurt like hell.

Five minutes later, it was all over and she announced, "We've removed the plaque. That'll be 1200 rupees."

So, I paid up, cursing myself for not studying hard enough in college to have been a dentist who could've charged people for scraping their teeth, and walked out. I couldn't help but feel that I'd been cheated out of something.

As soon as I stepped out, I saw the brilliance of the dentist's business plan – his clinic was right next to a bakery in which I could see breads and cakes and doughnuts calling out to me from within. Cursing my weak will, I went in and bought a fresh sugar doughnut and bit into it. Just as I was about to wipe the sugar crumbs off my lips, the short, stocky woman dentist walked into the same bakery, bought some sweets, gave me a knowing smile and walked out.

"Bastards," I said to myself as I walked back home, enjoying my doughnut.

#52: No, I Said Back!

I hate nymphomaniac married women.

I was on this train from Delhi to Bangalore, and I was sharing the compartment with a married family from Gwalior. There was the dad, the mum and the three-year-old stereotypical kid. She whined at all the right times and was cute at all the right moments. She smiled just enough to get her way and played mum and dad against each other as only kids can.

The journey wasn't very interesting apart from the midnight beer by the open door and the unhealthy yet tasty food all the way to Bangalore. But what was really um... interesting, was that the mum was quite hot. Hey, I'm not a man who goes after mums – no, I'm not that kind of man at all. In fact, mums usually like me for what I am – a soft-spoken, decent guy. I may have said too much, but I'll risk it. Bottom line is that I'm not a guy who goes after mums.

Anyway, there was this mum who was quite hot and looked quite disgusted with herself for having to tend to the kid. She kept giving me *Yeah-tell-me-about-it* kind of looks, rolling her eyes every time her kid asked her to pick her up, etc. She had a cute smile – the mum, not the kid – and she used it very well against me, and got me to close my novel and start a conversation.

She told me her story, and I told her mine. All this time, the dad was either sitting next to her and playing with the kid, or roaming around the train looking for water and food and other things. So, we were quite alone during most of our conversations. I tried my best not to be charming because then there would be no going back. I was just

[131]

coming out of an extremely ugly relationship back then and at that phase of my life, I considered all women to be – okay, let me not complete that. I respect women very much, I'm a feminist to the core, but I just wasn't desperate enough to start picking up hot moms on trains.

So, I told her about my situation and that I was going back to Bangalore. At that precise instance, the train passed over a bridge, changing the noise levels. I'm sure she heard me wrong, because her eyes opened wide for an instant, and then she looked down at the floor with a shy smile. I saw her blush furiously. I was confused. She looked up at me and said, in a hushed voice, "Here??" and gave a small, girly, giggle.

I was staring at her. I was thoroughly confused and asked her, "What? Here what?"

Her husband came back just then and that put an end to our conversation. She didn't talk to me at all for the next forty minutes, until she had to get off the train. She kept blushing and avoiding my eyes.

Only when she was getting off at this place called Mammad, did I realize what that incident was. She gave me a wink as she left, and it dawned on me. She had heard me say, "Want to jump in the sack?"

No, I'm not that kind of guy. Really!

#53: From Bangalore With Love

Strange things seem to happen to me most of the time. I don't know if anyone else experiences as much weirdness on a daily basis as I do. Today, a DHL courier guy sniffed my butt, I broke my thumb, and I managed to get myself locked in an ATM vestibule. All within a span of two hours.

I wanted to send a package to Kerala. It contained a couple of pretty dresses for a pretty friend (on whom I had had a crush for a while now), on the occasion of *Onam* (a traditional Hindu festival celebrated in Kerala). She had specifically asked me not to send anything, and that was why I had to send her something. So, after some confused shopping, I settled on a pair of *kurtas*. I vowed never to shop for women again.

In the evening, I left office a bit early to courier the package at the DHL office, which was just a few miles away. A harrowing one-hour ride in dirty traffic on my rickety bike later, I reached the place.

"Hi," I said to the courier guy sitting behind the desk. "I've got a package to be sent to Kerala."

"Sir, all connections to Kerala are closed for Onam. It'll reach only on Monday," he said.

I sighed and said, "Ok, fine. Give me the earliest connection," and tried to un-sling my backpack, but it wouldn't budge. There was an irritating hook in the bag, which had gotten stuck to my belt buckle and my bag was locked in place. When I tried to move it, my pants rode up, giving me a wedgie. It was quite embarrassing, and the courier guy was looking at me with some amusement.

"Excuse me," I told him. "Can you please help me with this hook? I think it's stuck to my pants." I was utterly, completely, thoroughly embarrassed and I hoped to hell he wouldn't recognize me on a later day.

He came around, stood behind me, crouched down and held his face as close to my butt as he dared. After a while, he said, "Yes sir, the hook is stuck to the belt buckle." He took a pair of scissors and bent down again. We struck a queer pose – me, standing there and him, bending down, examining my ass with a pair of scissors in hand. I was desperately hoping that no one would walk through the door and find the both of us in this compromising position. My prayers were answered, and soon, he had freed the hook from my pants and I could un-sling my bag. We avoided looking into each other's eyes.

"Can I pay with my credit card?" I asked as I handed over the package to him.

"No sir," he said. Of course not. Things can never be too easy, right? So, I told him, "Ok, then start billing, I'll go to the ATM next door."

Three people stood in a line outside the ATM, and I patiently waited for my turn. Ten excruciating minutes later, I finished my transactions and withdrew the money. As I tried to open the door, I realized that it was locked. The ATM vestibule had a button that was needed to be pushed in order to open it from the inside, and that button had been ripped out, with only a few dangerous-looking wires hanging loose from the hole. I didn't know what to do. There was no phone on the inside and my cell phone was dead.

I waited there for exactly nine minutes until someone else came up to the ATM. I told him that I was locked in and that he could open the door by inserting his card through the slot on the other side. He did so and I was free. I thanked him and together, we hauled a big rock and blocked the door so that it wouldn't shut completely, trapping some other poor fellow.

I ran up to the DHL office and paid the money, took my receipt and ran out. *Finally*, I said to myself. *I can go home in peace.*

As I was removing my bike from the parking lot, I dropped my helmet, which I was holding in my hand. Instinctively, I bent down to pick it up before it rolled away onto the main road, lost control of the bike and fell over to my side, with my left thumb being pinned between the concrete and the bike's handle. One tiny bone somewhere inside that thumb snapped and driving back in that pain was hell. I was screaming all the way home and people thought I was drunk.

From Bangalore, all the way to Kerala, with love. I hope they deliver the package to the right address!

#54: My Jodha

Only once in a lifetime do we get a chance to be swept off our feet and made to fall head over heels in love.

Of late, there's nothing exciting happening in my life that is worth writing about – last night, I was stranded in the middle of the road when my bike ran out of fuel and this morning, a download I had kept in progress overnight, crashed and I had to restart the process again, but all this is quite normal and I can only say that God was in an awfully playful mood the past week. But more than this, the terror-child Cupid has been pulling at my heart strings for a very long time, and has been forcing me to write this post.

I've been reading this fascinating book by Salman Rushdie called *The Enchantress Of Florence*, a book that was gifted to me by this very special woman. I don't want to be a clichè over and over again about her, but the heart rules the mind these days and I don't want my logical brain to come in the way.

In the book, Rushdie talks about the relationship between Akbar and his beloved Jodha, and she is portrayed as an imaginary woman, a Phantom Queen who pleases the emperor in all aspects and makes him ignore all his other queens, thus making them jealous of this figment of Akbar's imagination.

She remains elusive and intangible throughout, at times lovely and at times frustrating because of her inability to be seen. Jodha has been portrayed as the product of the emperor's fertile imagination, and remains the unseen whiff of wind, the unheard laugh, the untasteable kiss, the unfeeling yet-so-warm touch and the fragrance that isn't. She resides in his head and yet roams around the vast palace, she resides in his heart and yet sleeps next to him at night, she plagues his mind and yet keeps him healthy, she feels sad about not being alive and yet she's so full of life, she's the only woman the emperor ever loved and ironically, being unreal, she's his only anchor to reality.

The only difference between the Jodha in the book and *my* Jodha is that the woman I love is as real as you and me. She's my anchor to reality just as much as the figment of Akbar's imagination.

I'm just a hopeless, pathetic, over-optimistic romantic!

#55: The Butt-on Brigade

This post is for the person who gave me that screwball lecture on Global Warming.

I sat through a long discourse on global warming and how it'll affect the kind of clothes we wear on a daily basis. Apparently, the Earth is going to become too hot for us to wear clothes and we'd all be walking around butt-naked on the streets, sweating like pigs. Nudists are going to have a field day, however, but the rest of us lesser mortals will be forced to do something drastic to preserve whatever little decency we have.

From the Stone Age to the Information Age and the present Boob-age, we're hurtling towards an Ass-age. Strangely, this comes just before the next Ice Age, and the two pronunciations are not to be confused with. So, what do we do in this ex-ass-perating situation?

There will come a time when people's butts will become a taboo – as tabooed as the other "private" parts. Unfortunately, people will not share the same obsession they have for these parts today and we'll see them being bared in public. But the butt is going to be highly private. Someone will invent a Butt-Guard or a Butt-Off or something similar in all shapes and sizes and fake ones too, that will protect the butt from prying eyes. More than anything, these inventions will prevent ass lovers from their eye-candy.

These ass lovers will create a secret society called the 'Butt'on Brigade, and their main objective will be to beautify the backside through underground videos. Scores of people will be misled into joining the 'Butt'on Brigade and kids as young as 10 will be brainwashed and made to join. Law and order will fail against the sheer numbers of the Brigadiers and the kids will create their own version called 'Little Asses.'

And since all the truths about Global Warming would have been proven to be true, the Governments of all the countries will decide that they need to ignore the ominous signs again. Their anal logic would be: Lightning doesn't strike the same place twice, so why should Global Warming?

But their logic would turn out to be just that – anal. Global Warming would strike again, bringing an end to the Ice- and the Ass Age. The taboos would return to normal. We'd be flashing our butts in public again and hiding other parts.

If only this fucked-up version of the future were true. Unfortunately, it's just a dream. An ass-piration.

#56: Revenge of the Idiots

This incident happened sometime last year, and I still remember it vividly. Idiots are so hard to forget.

It was supposed to be a surprise. Or a suspense. Whichever one wasn't creepy. One hour was the time frame. I was supposed to present myself at the remote location in one hour. *Yeah, right,* I thought. *With this traffic, I can make it just in time for a perfect sunset.* Three in the afternoon on the roads of Bangalore is like being killed and transported to Hell and made to push a huge, heavy wheel for no apparent reason, with a red, pointy-tailed, French-bearded individual who laughs demonically for no reason lashes you with a whip every now and then – your sweat dripping off your body and crusts of dirt and tar sticking to every part of your face. Well, almost.

I was stuck in each and every traffic light on my way. The location was called BTM Layout, and I was cursing the fellow who'd called me there. While I waited for more than ten minutes at a junction where a truck was stranded in the middle of the road with two-wheelers peppered around it like seasoning on a horrendous Christmas dish, my mind went back to the phone call I had received that morning.

"Hey Nikhil," said the idiot over the phone.

"Hey dude," I replied, silently wishing he hadn't called. I hated this guy, and had tried to distance myself as much as possible from him. But some people just don't get it.

"Listen, this is important," said the Idiot. "Can I meet you today? This is really important!"

The Idiot had called me after a gap of almost three years and this is how he opened the conversation.

"Yeah dude, tell me," I said, sounding as indifferent as possible.

"Can you come to BTM Layout at 3.00 today? Please man, this is important!"

"Whoa!" I said. "What? It's a Sunday, if you remember? I'm trying to relax at home."

"Please Nikhil. I wouldn't call you if it weren't important. Please come to the mall in BTM and call me. I'll pick you up." No matter what I tried, he wouldn't give in. I finally agreed to meet him.

"Thanks a lot, man!" he said.

"No problem. This better be worth it."

"Oh, it is! It is! Don't you worry! Just be there at three and I'll pick you up," he said. "So, how've you been these past few years?"

"Bye dude. See you at three," I said and hung up. It's not that I'm an anti-social animal – I just hate this guy.

So here I was, stuck in inching traffic on a blisteringly hot Sunday, in the middle of nowhere, about to meet this Idiot, when I should've been at home, my feet up on the couch, leaning back in my sofa, watching the French Open finals with a chilled Coke in my hand. Ah, life mocks me. I can't help it.

I reached the place in one piece and my bike groaned to a halt as I parked her. The engine trickled as it cooled down. I loved my bike. She was a work of art. She belonged in a museum, under the "Tools of the Neanderthal" section.

I called up the Idiot and told him that I'd reached. It was two minutes to three. I sat back on my parked bike and waited for the Idiot. He arrived two minutes later, running, and hot in the face. He was a weird looking guy – tall and balding, with a thin hairline mustache. And his eyes were a constant reminder of his inborn idiocy. He had always been an idiot –

[141]

slow to grasp things and concepts and slower to understand them. Now, he was working for a software company. God save software!

"Thanks for coming, dude!" he said.

"No problem," I said. "Ok, what's this all about?"

"Listen, I'm into a scheme where you can make lots of money in a week. Up to twenty thousand in a week! Are you interested?"

You can imagine what went through my brain. I looked around for a sizable rock to bash his head in, but refrained myself. Too many witnesses around. I could never make it look like an accident.

"What?" I asked, incredulously.

"Yeah man! This new company is giving away money, dude. I asked you to come here because I want you to attend a presentation, which the company is giving. They'll explain exactly how you can make the money. It's quite simple, dude. And I get a referral fee if you sign up."

"What?" I asked again. I was beginning to eye some really nice rocks.

"Yes," he said. "Follow me."

He led me to a hotel which was behind the mall. Lots of people were hanging around the entrance. "These are all my colleagues," he said.

"Ok," I said. I was really annoyed now, as most of the people there had the same idiot look in their eyes. I wanted to run away from there as fast as I could. He led me into the hotel and into an air-conditioned conference room, where there was a long table, made of cheap wood to match the cheapness of the wood-paneled walls. Lots of people were sitting around it and there was a whiteboard on the far wall, with a guy standing in front of it.

"Guys, this is Nikhil," said the Idiot. They all waved at me. I was asked to take the only empty chair in the room, while the Idiot stood by the wall. I felt like the newest inductee into the Idiot Club of India.

The presentation started. Two minutes into the talk, I hated the Idiot all the more. We were supposed to pay thirty thousand rupees to join the "company," and then go out and refer more people and convince them to join the same charade. Every time one of the poor idiots joined, we would get a commission. And just to show that the company believed in proper "motivation," we would be given a gold coin once we pay them the initiation fees. If there is one thing I hate more than Pyramid Schemes, it's the people who run them.

I frantically took out my cell phone and texted a friend to call me, just so that I could get an excuse to get out of the place. He did, and I walked out, telling the Idiot that I had to attend the call. I went out, took a deep lungful of refreshing, polluted Bangalore air and told the Idiot who had followed me out that I was going home. "I'm not interested, dude. Honestly. I think it's not going to work. You want my suggestion? Quit," I told him.

"Hey, it's ok dude. It's really your choice. Are you sure you don't want the gold coin?"

I wanted to bash his head in badly, but I summoned all my inner strength and held back. Oh, I hated him.

"Bye, dude," I said. "Don't ruin my Sunday again."

As I rode back, I felt sorry for the scores of idiots fooled in this quest for money. Greed had blinded them so much that they could believe almost anything. I went back home and splashed my face with cold water. I switched on the fan, lay back on the sofa, put my feet on the couch with my chilled Coke, and switched on Star Sports. Roger Federer had just won the first set. I settled back with a contented sigh, when the power went out.

Life mocks me.

Sometimes, when I hear closely, I think I can hear the crack of a whip and a demonic laugh.

#57: Heads Up! The True Story Of Why I Quit Journalism

Finally, I am strong enough to reveal the truth. This incident took place in the offices of a leading daily newspaper in the city. None of what follows is fiction. Unfortunately, and gruesomely, every word of it is true. This is definitely not for the faint of heart.

I am a little apprehensive about sharing this incident with you all, but then, it's about time I set the record straight and confess to everyone why I quit journalism.

I'll try to report exactly what happened, objectively and without any emotional bias. Oh, who am I kidding? I'm going to tell you exactly what happened. Trust me, this is scary.

It was 2.00 in the morning, and the office was deserted. I was on the night shift, and had just finished a satisfying cigarette and was walking up the old staircase to my desk. There wasn't a soul anywhere in the huge building. The only sounds I could hear were those of the air-conditioner cranking up a notch and the occasional roar of a speed devil out on the road. There was a chill in the night air, and I hugged myself for warmth and entered the office. If I stood still and strained my ear, I could hear the footfalls of the people walking on the pavement outside. I glanced at my watch and decided it was high time I packed up and went home for the day. Being on the internet/technology desk of a newspaper isn't a comfort. More than anything, it's a hindrance. Unfortunately for me, this newspaper was widely read, and I had to stay back till 2.00 in the morning to give our insomniac readers the latest update of who killed whom in the world.

I returned to my desk and started to close all the open windows in the computer. I switched off the AC and the muted television, where the cricket match of the day was being shown again. As I heard the satiating jingle of Windows shutting down, I switched off the monitor, picked up my bag, and stopped.

My bag seemed exceptionally heavy. I didn't remember bringing any books to work and I distinctly remember the bag being very light. Now, I noticed that there was a slight bulge in the bag's midsection. My bag was one of those horizontal zipper bags that require to be slung across the shoulder. These kinds of bags are great for carrying books, but are woefully inadequate for anything slightly bulkier, like water bottles and tiffin boxes. They stand out like a pregnant belly. There was a similar bulge in my bag. I was confused.

I looked down at the bag again and placed it back on the desk. Frowning, I opened the zipper and looked inside. I almost screamed out.

There, lying in a pool of dirty papers, was the most hideous looking head I've ever seen. And the fact that there was a *head* in my bag almost made me faint. It looked up at me with this horrendous expression. I couldn't speak, my mouth was dry and my heart was beating so furiously that I thought it was going to break free and run away. I wiped the sweat off my head and looked around to see if there was anyone who was watching me. There wasn't a soul.

I'm a pretty rational guy, and my mind quickly switched on the rationale. I started thinking of how this head could've gotten in my bag. Obviously, someone must've placed it there when I wasn't at my desk. Now, there were only two instances when I hadn't been at my desk the whole evening – once for dinner and once for my habitual 2.00 AM smoke break. I could rule out dinner, because the office had been packed more tightly than a circus at that time.

So, obviously, someone had put the head in my bag, when I was out smoking. This made me feel a bit frightened, as I was fairly sure that there wasn't anyone in the office.

Or was there?

[145]

I had goose bumps on my arms. A shiver ran down my spine. "Relax," I told myself. "There's no such thing as ghosts!"

"Yeah," replied my brain. "But there're serial killers and murderers and psychos!"

Now, I felt really scared. I am a well-built guy, and I could hold my own against anyone looking for a fight, but the thought of defending myself against a crazed lunatic who'd just dumped a fucking head in my bag? Well, I frankly preferred the quiet life.

The phone rang on my desk, suddenly and shrilly, making me jump out of my skin. The sound of the phone seemed unnaturally loud in the quiet office, and scarier with the head in my bag. I approached it gingerly and picked it up. I could hear my heart pounding against my chest.

"H-hello...?" I said.

"Nikhil?" came a gruff voice that I couldn't recognize.

"Yeah, who's this?" I demanded, slightly strung out, hoping that the person, whoever it was, wouldn't notice the tension in it.

"Are you alone?" the voice asked.

"What?" I asked, now scared. *"Who is this?"*

"Do you have the head?" the voice said.

I was terrified, and a bit angry. "Who the hell is this? And what's the meaning of this sick joke? *Whose head is this?"*

"Joke? Didn't you find my note?"

"What note? *Who the fuck are you?"*

"You don't recognize me, do you?" he asked.

"Obviously not, asshole!"

"Check the note next to your computer. *That head is mine*," he said, and the line got cut.

I held the dead receiver next to my ear for a long time with sweat running down my face, and finally put it down. I looked next to my computer and found a yellow post-it stuck on the side of the monitor. Why hadn't I noticed it earlier? Curiously, I pulled it out and read what was written on it.

I looked at the head in my bag and back to the note I was holding in my hand, and vowed never to do night shifts again. I couldn't take it anymore.

"*Nikhil,*" the note began, "*please find the head of cabbage in your bag. Keep it in a fridge and bring it tomorrow. I don't have a fridge at home. How was dinner? Thanks. Ranjit.*"

That asshole colleague of mine didn't even tell me! Imagine finding a head of cabbage in your bag when you least expect it! I am freaked out.

I resigned the next day. I prefer the quiet life. Without heads.

#58: The Hazards Of A Public Relations Occupation

And I thought working in a coal mine in Siberia was dangerous. Public Relations is a field which only the brave pursue and only those with a casual disregard for personal safety excel in.

When I signed on for a career in Public Relations, I knew it would involve daily death threats from irate clients and journalists, but I didn't expect bodily harm. For instance, there was this homosexual client called Mr. B, who was sleeping with the bisexual editor of a popular national newspaper and I wasn't supposed to tell this to anyone because they knew where I lived.

Yesterday was a gloomy Tuesday, with dark clouds threatening to douse the city, and a cold wind that seemed never-ending. I arrived a bit later than usual, courtesy the dirty traffic and a full bladder, and went about my work with the right mix of boredom and enthusiasm. It was sometime in the afternoon when I realized just how dangerous my line of work is.

I was sitting at my desk, reading an online news release, when I dropped my pen on the floor. As I bent to pick it up, the chair I was sitting on creaked a bit. I didn't give it much thought as it had always creaked. Just as my fingertips touched the floor, I heard a deafening *crack* and the damn chair snapped in three. I fell down on the floor quite awkwardly, with a heavy thud. The entire office was silent and I lay there, dazed, wondering what in the hell had happened.

Slowly, people realized something was wrong and crowded around my cubicle. They helped me to my feet and made me stretch just to make sure that nothing was broken. More than embarrassment, I was angry at a friend of mine who had me following a diet which clearly wasn't working!

I realized a bit later that I had cut my thumb quite deeply during the fall. I don't know how that happened, and my butt ached painfully all through the day. That I am accident prone is an understatement.

My bike ran out of fuel on my way back and I had to push it for half an hour, bearing the painful butt and the cut finger, and then stopped for another half an hour waiting for my friend to arrive and rescue me with some petrol. During that wait, I almost ate a dirty omlette from a street cart but refrained from it after seeing the "cook" scratch his balls and his armpits and wipe his hands on a dirty *lungi* before picking up the omlette with his hands and dropping it on to someone else's plate – who ate it with gusto.

I think that this story will be enough to make people looking for a career in Public Relations think twice and thrice before embarking on the most dangerous job in the world.

#59: The Banana Run

banana [**buh-nan-uh**]

–noun

1. A tropical plant of the genus Musa, certain species of which are cultivated for their nutritious fruit.

2. The fruit, esp. that of M. paradisiaca, with yellow or reddish rind.

One of the more fascinating aspects of being cooped up in a room that stinks worse than a ten-year-old freshly dug-up coffin is the ease with which we can find blackened banana skins in the most unexpected places. I found seventeen last night.

My brother doesn't clean his room. Ever. I think the last time the room faced the business end of a broom and a mop was when it was built, more than a thousand years ago. We exchanged rooms for the night as he said he had to prepare for an exam and needed the computer all night. My guess is as good as yours – I found three porn sites in the internet history later. But anyway, I don't want to digress into a 19-year-old's late night exploits.

Entering his room is akin to stepping out of civilization and entering a Neanderthal realm of sabre-tooth tigers, mammoths, man-eating men and rotting food. I stepped into a half-eaten box of ice cream lying on the floor, as soon as I entered the room. This should've warned me what to expect, but I blissfully ignored it and crept into the bed. It was unusually warm and cozy.

Unfortunately, the warmth was due to the fact that the bed was partly drenched with fresh hot coffee, and I hadn't noticed it in the darkness. I changed the sheets and crept in again, and realized that the pillow seemed to emanate a strange smell that distinctly reminded me of the frog dissections I used to do in school. And there it was, under the pillow, nestled snugly, the first of the blackened banana skins.

I realized that I couldn't sleep unless I was satisfied that nothing else was hidden in the bed. I stripped the bed of all sheets and turned over the mattress, and immediately, cursed myself for doing so. In the midst of a couple of cockroach corpses and old newspapers and new porn magazines, I found sixteen more banana skins.
I spent the night in the living room, on the couch – safer and a lot wiser.

I got a pounding from the creep the next morning for destroying the chaotic sanctity of his room. A great start to the day.

#60: Towards A Greater Kiss

Mercurians, Venutians, Martians and Earthlings have all gotten together and have voted me as the *Best Kisser In The Solar System* after 49 grueling hours of tongue-wrestling contests, elections, re-takes and encores. To my surprise, everyone there referred to me as *The Love Guru*, which made me feel all the more better about the whole deal. I returned to Earth this morning, feeling quite happy about myself.

A kiss is something surreal that only two people get to experience at any given time. A great kiss isn't planned – it's spontaneous. It elevates the participants to a whole new level, much above the clichéd cloud nine. Contrary to popular belief, a kiss doesn't just involve the lips and the tongue – the whole body, mind and soul play vital roles in making a good kiss great.

A kiss is not just an acronym, it's something much more. It's perhaps the greatest discovery by Earthlings after the wheel. It's interesting to record what actually goes on in the minds of two people when they kiss – more often than not, it's nothing. The mind's blank. Nothing goes in or out of the brain and all electrical activities come to a standstill. Instinct takes over reason. Irrationality takes over common sense.

False starts and awkward poses are always a part of the game. We have to think beyond that. We have to think about the sweet taste, the soft wetness and the overwhelming head rush. We, as human beings, are constantly held up in a mad race for money and time is running short. There're a lot of things we can do that doesn't cost money, that lets us experience a far higher sense of satisfaction than materialistic goods.

I say, start with a kiss.

#61: The Airport Taxi From Hell

There is mystery in the air. Stop whatever you're doing and sniff the air around you. If you can ignore the fish and the next guy's sweat, you can smell the mystery in the air. I know I can. I think I am being followed by an airport taxi. Everywhere I go and everywhere I turn, there's an airport taxi lurking nearby. I think there is a conspiracy afoot, and yesterday, I thought about it long and hard and I have a feeling that I've hit upon the truth.

Once upon a time, I was in love with a strange girl from Hawaii. Her name was Yu Suk, and she was perhaps the third most beautiful woman in the world. We loved each other very much and though we were separated by more than 5000 miles of ocean, we believed that one fine day we would be together and live happily ever after. The long-distance relationship proved to be arduous, however, and drained the both of us completely. I decided to end it. That's when *she* decided to fly down to Bangalore and meet me and show me just how much she loved me. I was over the moon!

I dressed up in my favorite yellow tee-shirt and blue jeans and rode all the way to the airport on the day. I reached an hour early and paced up and down, waiting for Yu Suk to arrive. I could hardly stand still in my excitement. I was nervous and feeling a bit horny at the same time. I guess it was natural.

Finally, the flight monitor indicated that her flight from Hawaii had landed and that the passengers were at the customs line. I was waiting right in front of the exit gate, standing behind the ubiquitous group of white-uniformed taxi drivers who were holding up cardboard placards with the names of their guests. Slowly, one by one, the passengers from Hawaii walked out into the bright Bangalore sun, shielded their eyes from the glare and searched for their respective receptions.

The taxi driver in front of me was chatting with his colleague next to him about his wife. He was saying, "What can I do, brother? She just cannot be satisfied every night. I feel she's draining me out!"

To this, his colleague replied, "You want some help, brother?" and winked and they both burst out laughing. I cringed at the crassness of their conversation, but couldn't help overhearing it. The first driver continued, "If anyone, *anyone*, mentions the S-word again, I'll kill them personally!" and they both started guffawing heartily. I just figured that the guy was totally and completely asexual and pitied his wife.

Just then, in the throng of the crowd, I saw her! There she was! Graceful and beautiful and as sexy as ever – wearing her favorite yellow tank top over a flowery knee-length skirt that flowed all around her. Her face was the embodiment of all the love and lust in the world – the high cheekbones, the sexy blue-green eyes, the straight black hair that fell in small fluffy curls just below her shoulder, those petite hips, those firm breasts, those long beautiful eyelashes, oh, I was so much in love!

She looked around her, scanning my waiting crowd from her moving crowd, looking for me, searching for the face of her lover. I waved my hand frantically and called out to her, "Yuuuuuuuuu Suuuuuuuuuuuuuk!"

I started running towards her in slow motion. The crowd around me dissolved into fields of poppies, with butterflies fluttering around, the sun shining down with its golden rays dripping with love, drenching the two of us in that moment of ecstasy. Her face broke into a beautiful smile as she saw me and she ran towards me in slow motion, through our very own field of poppies. I held out my arms to embrace her, and she held out her arms to run into mine. At that moment, I felt something hard hit me on the back of my head and I tripped over myself and fell face-down on the hard concrete floor of the airport. The field of poppies and the butterflies disappeared and I could just see dazed stars all around me for a few moments.

I was aware of two distinct voices – one angry and one concerned – around me. I looked up and saw Yu Suk arguing with a taxi driver. It was the guy who had been standing in front of me, discussing his wife. I sat up and rubbed the back of my head and saw an old, heavy boot lying next to me. He had thrown a boot at me! That bastard!

"Hey!" I cried standing up. "What the fuck were you thinking throwing shoes at people?" I geared up for a fight.

"You bastard!" he cried. "You abused me verbally!"

I was confused. "Eh, what? When did I do that? Stop talking nonsense!"

"Shut up, you punk! You said, 'You Suck!' so loudly that the whole bloody airport heard it!"

So, thus began a hatred, rooted in miscommunication that spanned the better half of the next decade – a decade that involved a lot of stalking, prank calls, threatening calls and three trips to the police station and one to the hospital. It got so bad that the cops finally had to request me to stop beating him up every time I saw him. I reluctantly agreed and made a deal with the bastard – I'd leave him alone if he accepted that it wasn't my fault to begin with. He was lying with three broken bones in the hospital bed, covered in bandages from head to toe, when he agreed. I could see hatred in his eyes.

It's been four years since I've heard from him or seen him, and recently, I think I scratched his car by mistake while I was parking my bike near the office. I did not notice the number of the car, but I am damn sure it was him, because when I came back after work, my bike wouldn't start – there were sugar lumps in the petrol tank and both my tires were flat.

I began noticing his car everywhere I went – the bastard is stalking me. I think it's time I reminded him who the better man is. I think it's time for him to visit the hospital again.

[155]

#62: Characteristics Of An Asshole

Some people are born losers. In my book, they fall into the category of assholes. I've written letters to them and ranted about them before, but they never fail to come back and beg me for more. Let me spend a few sentences defining this unique class of people.

Assholes are all around us, living normal lives in the guise of normal people. They will smile at you, laugh with you, hang out with you for a few beers, and when the time is right, ask you for a lot of money. Well, it's not usually the money, but more often than not, they'll ask you for money when you're broke and when you'd rather kill someone for some excitement in life. Assholes are those people you'd much rather block in your chat groups and social networking sites. Assholes are those people who are stored as "Moron" or "That Guy" in your phone, whose call you'd much rather ignore.

Assholes are people who have a stupid look in their eyes all the time and they never fail to annoy everyone around them with their constant stream of daft moments. Assholes are men, women and children who have either been dropped on their heads as kids or have been at the receiving end of scandalous posts like these. Assholes have been written about in books and sung about in songs and pushed around on the streets.

Assholes are God's way of giving us the much-needed confidence in ourselves and our stupidity, which is always overshadowed by theirs. We tend to live our lives in the happy conclusion that we're geniuses and that people like Einstein and Tesla were but an anomaly. We become over-confident in our subtlety and never fail to obfuscate our decisions with our doubts when we're around assholes. They scream into our ear for a pittance of importance and usually are pity-sponges. Oh, I've known a lot of assholes in my life. Too many, in fact.

If you can't spot the asshole in your social circle, then it's probably you.

#63: Valentine's Day: A Cynical Deconstruction

It's finally here. The Day of Love. Loads of people around the world get married on this day, conceive their first-born kids on this day, break up and commit suicide on this day. I find the last two facts more fascinating, for purely statistical reasons.

I have been known to write extensively on the subject of love, talking constantly about my girlfriends, praising their beauty and snubbing their stupidity, proclaiming my life-long love for a few and announcing my denouncement of a few. I have given advice to single men and women on how to pick up members of the opposite sex and I have given advice on how to break up without compelling the other person to kill themselves or worse, commit murder. But this year, in glorified 2011, I have decided to change tracks and expound on the disadvantages of being in love, the utter stupidity of having a "Day" to express your feelings and cynically deconstruct the notion of paradise.

I am not doing this out of spite. No. On the contrary, it's taken me twenty-seven years to understand the true nature of relationships, the flimsy, see-through negligée that people cloak their statuses with. Never have I been this clear about my thoughts and feelings. Never have I been this single.

I don't like it one bit – the whole world waiting for one stupid day on which, eons ago, some poor fucker with the unfortunate name of Valentine was burned at the stake. There have been stories written about this day, books published, movies made and documentaries shot, and all of them talk about the same lousy thing – if you love someone, you'll pop the question on V-day. *Bullshit*. If you love someone, you don't need a "Day" to do it. After all, it's a fantastic excuse to get laid. Apart from this, I don't think this day has any other relevance. I pity the poor unborn souls who get conceived each year on this day – they are either a drunken mistake, a sober mistake or a mistake of faulty contraception. A mistake, nonetheless.

I hate it when people text me asking who my "Valentine" is. I feel like slapping the crap out of them and wishing them a Happy Valentine's Day. Of course, I can't do that. Or maybe I should. Ending up in jail on assault charges seems to be the best thing to happen to me on this day. I'll be spared the nonsense that wraps the world in a dense web of stupidity, pointlessness and vague references to a vague concept called "Love."

Note to Cupid: Die, asshole.

Author's Note: I currently love Valentine's Day. It gives me an opportunity to shower gifts on my beautiful wife and get laid. I think it's the best day of the year. I only hated it when I was single, just like you did when you were single. High five, fucker!

#64: The Boy And His Stuffed Tiger

He opened his eyes to darkness. He felt around with his hands and found the wall to his right, along which his bed lay. He groped around until he found a switch and flipped it on. Harsh white fluorescent light filled the room and hurt his eyes. Reflexively, he closed them and groaned. His head hurt – no, pounded – from within, and it felt like a million sledgehammers were threatening to break open his skull. He turned on to his side and winced as sharp points of pain pricked his joints and when he couldn't take it anymore, he sat up. Still dressed in his clothes from the night before, he looked down at his hands and feet, wondering how he ever got home. The last thing he remembered was his tenth beer. There had been a lot of shouting, a lot of music – loud music, and a lot of beer. He vaguely remembered throwing up somewhere, and sure enough, he saw the dirty yellow stains on his white shirt and blue jeans. "Shit," he muttered, and swung his legs off the bed.

Standing in the middle of the room, he stretched himself and took a step towards the bathroom when he stepped on something soft and furry. He looked down at the old stuffed tiger he used to play with as a kid, and kicked it under the bed in anger. He had suffered enough because of it, and he had no intention of ruining his life further.

"Twenty years," he said to the bit of furry tail still visible from under the bed. "Twenty years of my life ruined because I thought you were real. They stuck me in a nut house and asked me to swallow pills every two hours. I don't know what I was thinking." Then, calming himself, he took a few deep breaths and said, almost chanted, "You're not real. You're not real."

He walked into the bathroom, showered, shaved and came out feeling refreshed. As he stood looking at his thirty-year old beaten, worn-out, pot-bellied frame in the mirror on the wardrobe door, he thought back to the day in his youth when he had burned his parents alive. The tiger had asked him to do it. The tiger had said it would be a good idea. He had listened to the tiger and killed his parents. Pain wracked through his mind and he shut his eyes tight as tears rolled down his wet cheeks. "I'm sorry," he said to no one in particular. He was different then, before the medication, before the doctors, before the black-outs.

When he turned away from the mirror and bent down to grab a shirt from the floor, he stopped dead in his tracks. The stuffed tiger that he had kicked under the bed was now back where it had been. The single remaining beady eye and the empty socket where the other bead had been, looked up at him in a cold stare, unflinching, as if daring him to talk. As if daring him to scream, to shout, to say something. He stared at the tiger, frozen in mid-step and too scared to do anything. He swallowed a large gulp of fear and said, "You're not real. You're not real. You're not real."

He turned away closing his eyes and shut both his ears with his hands, still chanting his mantra. When he stopped to catch a breath, he heard someone call his name from behind him.

"Calvin," the voice said. "Why won't you talk to me anymore?"

"No!" he screamed. "Don't talk to me! You're not real!" He was still turned away, now crouching near the wall, his head resting against the corner. "Shut up!"

"You think I don't miss you, Calvin?" the voice asked.

"You're not real. You're not real..." he continued in monotone, rocking back and forth, drowning out the tiger's voice.

"Of course I'm real. I'm right here. Turn around, Calvin."

He didn't know why he did it, but he did. He turned, opened his eyes and saw the tiger standing there in the middle of the room. The tiger was smiling at him, standing on its hind legs, holding out its hands as if waiting for an embrace. Calvin took a tentative step towards the tiger, still confused and the madness showing on his face with no inhibition. "No!" he screamed. "You are NOT real!" and he ran towards the bed-side drawer, pulled out a gun from inside and put the barrel in his mouth.

He looked at the tiger's eye and saw the tears rolling down to its cheek and forming tiny puddles on the floor. He was crying himself. He couldn't stop the tears.

"Don't do it, Calvin," said the tiger, stifling a sob.

"I'm sorry, Hobbes," he said and pulled the trigger. As the last shard of life left his body, he thought he saw a stuffed tiger lying at his feet. He tried to smile and tried to tell himself that the tiger was not real. He tried, in vain.

#65: If You Hate Someone

Of all the things I hate the most, I think I hate being talked about behind my back. Well, I know I can't escape it, but when things are said without being thought through and without any consideration for the consequences, it irks me to no end. Oh, I'm not angry right now, as I write this. I am just wondering about the two fundamentals of human emotion – love and hate. Isn't it strange how you can love a person one instant and hate them the next? Of course, it's a well-known dichotomy that people live with, but when it hits you in the face, you can't help but wonder about the fragility of everything that was and everything that could have been.

Why the hell am I ranting so much? Does the asshole I'm referring to even realize that I'm ranting about him?

Anyhoo, here's the situation – I met an asshole in Bombay, who single-handedly made my week miserable and got away with it. I'm not a revenge-seeking-guy and I don't really care about what happens to the asshole from now on. For all I care, the asshole can stand in the middle of the road butt-naked and punch a speeding bus in the face. But, interestingly enough, I realized that the asshole was just doing his job.

Most assholes are just doing their jobs, and in the process, they piss you off. From the goodness of my heart, I will excuse the bastard and let him lead his miserable excuse of a life. But here's an open invitation to anyone who reads this: If you hate someone, and you want me to slander that person in my own fantastic way, then send me an email with the asshole's name (or a fake name, I don't care), his/her gender and the reason why you hate him/her. I will not disappoint you.

#66: Things To Do Before I Die

No, this isn't just any other bucket list. This one's unique.

There are quite a few bucket lists floating around on the internet. I've seen and read them all, and most of them follow a predictable formula – go traveling somewhere, see some sights, taste some foods, etc. That's all fine and dandy, and I wish them all the best in their endeavors. I have a few of those things to do as well, but I don't think they would qualify for my bucket list. For example, I'd love to see a sunset over the Grand Canyon someday and I would give a hand and a foot to see the insides of a Pyramid. But these are things that I can and will do over the next few years. What I would ideally put in my bucket list are unconventional things that one would not normally find in conventional bucket lists.

Here's my list.

1. I want to see the DNA molecule. Not the vague, hazy white mass that appears at the bottom of a test tube after centrifugation, no. I want to see the molecule in all its double-helical glory. I don't think anyone has. Ever.

2. I want someone to come up with a concrete explanation for the nature of light. I think Newton was confused enough to propose two theories that fit his math better. If light is a wave, then one equation works and if light is made up of particles, then the other equation works. I don't think I'm alone when I say that both these schools of thought were born out of necessity than reality. I want to see a solid unifying explanation before I die.

3. I want to travel around the world in eighty days without flying. If Jules Verne can do it (or his character, at least), then so should I. Yeah, I know, this isn't exactly a wow-event, but it'd be cooler than seeing the Eiffel Tower. And without flights, it'd be double the fun.

4. I want to be able to sit on my porch with my dog on a Monday morning, put my feet up, open a can of cold beer, and shoot trespassers with birdshot. Redneck for a day.

5. So far, in all my twenty-seven years, there has been only one book that has made me go, "Oh wow!" at the end – Italo Calvino's *If On A Winter's Night A Traveler*. I want to read three more such books before I die.

6. There are seven people I know whose lives I want to ruin. I think I should be able to do that without too much trouble. I'm not a scheming psychopath. I just think that these seven people deserve a lot worse for all the lives they have ruined.

One fine day, I'm going to buy a house in Gokarna and settle down there. What would make life more interesting at that point of time is owning a nice big tavern on the ground floor.

One day at a time.

#67: Hunger Strike

We Indians have a peculiarly unique way of demanding justice. We stop eating and call for a press conference.

It all started with the great Mahatma Gandhi, who went on a hunger strike to oppose the tyranny of the British Raj, back in the 1930s and 1940s. This habit did not die after we got our independence. Every time the government does something that someone doesn't approve of, a hunger strike is called for along with a press conference.

Recently, an old fucker called *Anna Hazare* did it to oppose all the corruption in the government. He was hailed as the present-day "Mahatma" and the media fell over themselves to draw parallels with him and the original. The fuckers called it the New Freedom Struggle. And more recently, a guy who made his living doing yoga, *Baba Ramdev* (another fucking lunatic), went on a hunger strike and no one knew why. I'm sure he gave a laundry list of reasons for doing what he did, but no one really understood them.

It's like an infectious disease here in India. If one person goes on a hunger strike, it spreads like a virus on heat and before you know it, your neighbor's on a hunger strike against the local corporation demanding better roads and clean water. It's about time I joined in the fun.

I am going on a hunger strike from today to oppose hunger strikes all over.

I will eat obscene amounts of food and go on a strike against hunger until everyone stops their respective hunger strikes and eradicates the country of this ridiculous disease. I vow to not go hungry again until my objective is fulfilled. This hunger strike will prove to the whole country that I am quite serious. I will not end this hunger strike until all hunger strikes have ended in this country.

I am ready for my title now. I prefer something cool, and nothing with the word "Mahatma" in it. That's become clichéd.

#68: How To Spot An Indian

I've been hearing about a lot of incidents of racial profiling, where Indians are "randomly" pulled out of lines at airports for a thorough check. It has picked up tremendously after 9/11 and I'm not surprised. As Indians, we unfortunately share skin color and hair styles of the usual terrorist suspects. I would be racially profiling myself, if I said that all terrorists are middle-eastern, so I won't say it.

A lot of people in Western countries shit their pants when they see a brown guy sporting a full beard. This fear is doubled if the brown guy is wearing a white *kurta*. And they practically run for their lives if this guy sports a *Taqiyah* – the traditional Muslim prayer cap. And there have been a few instances where white guys literally have had heart attacks when the brown guys they had been talking to, used the word "Allah" in their sentences.

This is so ridiculous. There is a limit to paranoia, and taking it out on brown-skinned men and women, just because some brown assholes killed a bunch of white people in the past, is calling for trouble. Don't get me wrong, I am shocked and disgusted each time there is a terrorist attack anywhere in the world. As a pacifist myself, I find the unnecessary loss of human lives intolerable. It is okay to be afraid, but it is not okay to assume that every guy with brown skin is a terrorist with a bomb strapped to his balls.

So, I have decided to write a small but useful guide to help people identify Indians in a line-up.

Look, Indians are a harmless, gutless bunch of people who gave the world *Kama Sutra*, and wanted everyone in the world to live happily together, having awesome sex with each other. We are not the kind of people who would want to harm others. Hell, we go ballistic when our kids eat non-vegetarian foods and call them murderers – we believe in instilling guilt very early in our kids.

The first thing you should notice about an Indian guy in a line-up (I'll get to Indian women later) is that he won't smile. His passport photo will look as if he is attending his mother's funeral. But this alone will not help you weed out Indians from terrorists, because terrorists don't smile in their passports either, as Russel Peters very eloquently put it a few years ago. So, the next thing to do is check out a suspect's Facebook profile or, if he's in the airport check-in / check-out line, grab his phone and check the pictures in his album. Here's what you will expect to see:

1. If the suspect in question is a student at an American / UK / Australian university, he will have definitely stored pictures of himself posing in front of every tree, post-box, car and white guy he came across. And in all these pictures, he will be wearing a pair of sunglasses that are too big for his face, the thickest fur-lined jacket (if it's winter) or a hat that can only be described as a fedora (if it's summer). He will also have the smuggest expression on his face that seems to say, "Look at me, I'm so bloody cool!" Yeah, he's an Indian, let him go. He will probably wet himself if he is questioned about bombs and guns.

2. If the suspect is older and his passport lists him as being married, then his phone / Facebook profile will have hundreds of photographs with his wife, taken on their wedding day – the wife will be posing solo in many of these, in a gaudy silk *sari* and a head-full of flowers, in front of various background images of waterfalls and mountains, arms raised in different gracious angles. He's an Indian, let him go.

3. If the suspect is older but unmarried, he will probably be trying to smuggle booze and cell phones out of the country to distribute to his cousins and friends and parents. Hold him, but be warned that he will have a fantastic defense planned – something about being

forced into this by a girlfriend or a dying kid from the Make-A-Wish Foundation.

I hope that these guidelines will keep law enforcement officials from profiling Indians because of their skin color. Always remember, we are the assholes posing stupidly in photographs. We are not killers.

It's quite easy to spot an Indian woman – she's very hot and she screams in terror when any guy gets too close.

#69: The Day I Turned Ninety

Author's Note: Oooh, 69!

Saturday, November 26, 2011 will always remain etched in my memory as a historic occasion, a day to remember and revere as I try to live out the remainder of my days painfully. I aged dramatically that day and it reminded me of *The Last Crusade*, where the bad guy drinks from the wrong cup and turns into an aged, shriveled skeleton in a matter of seconds.

It was a really bad decision to play a professional cricket match with no practice.

I used to play a lot of cricket as a kid. I played for the school and college teams and garnered a bit of pro experience here and there. I wasn't a great cricketer, but I wasn't too bad either. I could hold my own against the real professionals. But, it's been an awfully long time since I've played competitive, professional cricket, and I've been woefully out of touch and shape. I have put on a few extra kilos around the middle and I don't move as quickly as I used to. I had completely forgotten what a grueling ordeal it is to be out on a cricket field on a hot and humid day for six hours.

As I started with my warm-up stretches in the morning, I wondered whether the exercises had become tougher over the past few years. I soon realized that my body was resisting it after being accustomed to comfortable couches and soft beds. I forced myself to finish the workout and to my horror, found out that the match had already started, that my team was batting first and that I was to bat at Number

3. For those who are uninitiated in the sport of cricket, if you're third in the batting order, then you go out to bat as soon as the first wicket falls.

I padded up in a hurry, went out to bat when the first wicket fell and was clean bowled first ball. I didn't seem to notice the ball zooming past my bat and my sluggish head was still trying to decide what to do about it, while I made the long walk back to the pavilion.

When it was our turn to bowl, I shuttled from one end of the field to the other after each over and by the time we were halfway through, I was ready to drop dead. I prayed for a natural disaster to disrupt the match, I prayed for the opposition to knock off the runs quickly and I prayed for an excuse that would allow me to get off the field with a feigned injury.

By the end of the day, after we had lost spectacularly, my feet were beyond pain and I had to remove my shoes and carry them with me as I hopped painfully into a cab to come back home. My entire body was one big bruise. I ached in places I didn't know could ache. Muscles that I didn't know I had, hurt each time I did something trivial. It was painful for me to spray deodorant on myself because my finger hurt when I pressed the nozzle-thingy on the can.

The whole of the next day was spent in recuperating at home, in bed, with timely cups of hot tea.

Saturday, November 26, 2011. The day I stopped being twenty-eight. The day I turned ninety.

#70: Great Egg-spectations

Of all the curious things I've noticed about Mumbai, one that stands out is the love this city has for eggs. Everywhere I go, I see carts laden with egg cartons and guys standing behind it, making omlettes and *burji* and toast. I come from the South, and people don't really like eggs down there. Very rarely do I come across an egg cart in Bangalore. Over here, if you throw a stone in the air, it is bound to land on an egg.

I walked up to one of these egg carts the other evening and ordered an omelette sandwich. As I munched on the little piece of heaven that seemed to melt in my mouth, I heard a voice behind me say, "You're Nikhil, aren't you?"

It was a woman's voice and it sounded a bit angry, laden with attitude. My hand was frozen midway between the plate and my open mouth as I turned to face the voice. It was a strange sight that met me. A withered, old, toothless woman stood there grinning, with a heavy plastic bag in one hand and an empty bucket in the other. She was draped in a heavy shawl, too heavy for the weather here in the city, and a pair of the thickest glasses perched on her nose. Her bat-like eyes stared at me from behind those glass walls and her toothless grin grew wider as I turned. She looked vaguely familiar.

"How you are, child?" she asked me in broken English and I realized who she was. She lived across the hallway from my apartment, had three kids, four grandkids, and was married to a filthy-rich younger guy, who was also the treasurer of our housing society. I had seen her around once in a while, when putting the garbage out or picking up my newspaper, and had smiled occasionally at her.

[173]

"I'm fine," I said giving her half a smile.

"Egg eating, are you?" she asked, pointing at my omlette sandwich with her chin.

"Yes."

"You eat egg at home, no?" she asked, suspiciously, furrowing her brows.

"Uhh, yes. I eat eggs at home," I said, wondering what her issue was and why she was even talking to me.

"Ok, now. You eat egg at home and *you do not throw egg shells in my kitchen!*" she yelled. "Throw egg shell in garbage, child," she added in a softer voice, with a smile and hobbled away down the road.

I stood there, stunned by her bipolar onslaught. I thought back to remember if I had ever thrown egg shells into her kitchen. Of course I hadn't. I keep to myself as a rule when living alone in a strange city, and I had no good reason, yet, to throw egg shells into my neighbors' houses.

So, that makes two curiosities in Mumbai that caught my attention so far – the love this city has for eggs and very eggcentric, crazy, old neighbors.

#71: The Christmas Nightmare

Every year, around Christmas, I am blessed with a nightmare or two about things that truly scare the shit out of me.

Very few things scare me as much as penguins do. Yeah, it's a rare phobia to have, and I am one of those very few people in the world who are afraid of the flightless fucking demons. They are evil and they won't hesitate to kill you and eat you, every chance they get. They walk like they are on a mission to hunt you down and their stare is enough to turn your blood cold.

Last evening, I had one of my frequent penguin nightmares. But it wasn't anything out of the ordinary. I dreamt that I was being hunted by a penguin dressed as Santa Claus.

I found myself in a strange room with three doors and no windows. A loud, disembodied voice called out to me, "Ho! Ho! Ho! Nikhil!"

More intrigued than scared, I looked around the room frantically to locate the voice. From somewhere, a draft of cold air blew through me and I shivered involuntarily. That's when I realized I was naked. There were absolutely no clothes on me at all. I tried to search for the source of the breeze but couldn't find any. There were no windows, as mentioned, and no vents or cracks in the wall. There was no furniture, no electric sockets or appliances of any kind. Despite the lack of light bulbs or any other artificial sources of light, the bare room was strangely illuminated in natural light. I wondered what the hell was going on.

"Ho! Ho! Ho!" came the voice again. It was a deep, guttural voice that was a bit menacing.

"Santa?" I whispered.

"Have you been a good boy this year?" asked the voice in a lilting tone, as if daring me to say yes.

"Wh- What? Yes! Yes, I've been a good boy!" I stammered, now thoroughly scared. I could feel my bladder filling up.

"Liar!" screamed the voice. "You're a liar!"

"No, No! I swear!" I yelled back.

Then, the door on the far right flew open with a bang and I couldn't see beyond the darkness of the doorway.

"Run," said the voice simply.

I stood there, frozen on the spot. Where was I? What was going on? I took a gingerly step towards the open door when the door on the far left flung open and there, framed in the dark doorway, stood a penguin, three and a half feet tall, wearing a blood-red Santa hat and brandishing a gleaming knife. It had a sneer on its face that almost seemed to tell me that my time was up.

It waddled towards me in the sinister way that penguins do, and spoke in the same creepy, bone-chilling voice, "I said, run."

Then came the laugh. The laugh that echoed all over the room, penetrated deep into my very soul and made my balls shrivel up into tiny dots. The laugh that seemed to cut open my skin and suck all my blood out. The laugh that echoed all around me and inside me and threatened to rupture my brain. The laugh that forced some feelings into my frozen legs and made me break into a run through the open door on the right, away from those menacing, blood-shot eyes of the crazy bird-beast.

I ran, sweating and panting and unable to scream or shout out for help. I ran as fast as I could in the darkness, not knowing where I was headed or where I was stepping. I could hear the pitter-patter of the beast's tiny flippers chasing after me. I could still hear it laughing as it ran, as if the beast were toying with me.

"Run faster, Nikhil," it called out to me. "Is that the best you can do?"

I could feel the voice growing louder which could only mean one thing. *The penguin was gaining on me!* I increased my speed and felt my lungs burning for oxygen. Every muscle in my out-of-shape body ached and screamed in pain as I forced my legs to work faster.

"Merry Christmas, Nikhil!" said the penguin-beast and laughed out one last time. I could feel the cold steel on my leg. *It had caught up to me and was slashing at my legs!* I found my voice and screamed out loud.

I woke up, drenched in sweat. I saw a Santa hat lying on the floor next to my bed, the hat that I had purchased from a roadside vendor that very same afternoon, in my misguided Christmas cheer. I glanced at my clock and saw that it was almost time to wake up. I swung my legs off the bed and stood up, snatched up the Santa hat and threw it in the dustbin. I put the trash out and made sure that someone picked it up and recycled the bloody thing.

Merry Christmas, you say? I'd say it's a fascinating start so far! Even now, I sit here and wonder: what might have been behind the middle door, the one that stayed shut?

#72: For The Last Time

You've been with me for seven years. We've held each other closer than anything else in the world. I've cared for you more than I've cared for myself. Or anyone else. I have loved you more than you can imagine. And you have given me such pleasure I can only dream about.

When we first started out, we were hesitant, unsure of how we would survive with each other. We hid our relationship from the world. Except one or two people, no one knew about us. We were careful, we tiptoed around the parents and the well-wishers. We gradually progressed into being much more than a casual fling. We became partners in life's grand journey. I carried you through some tough times and you did the same to me.

All those days and wonderful nights when you comforted me and gave me so much pleasure are fresh in my memory. We've laughed, cried, drank, sang, danced, played and slept together. We have been each other's best friends and the worst enemies. We have been each other's best lovers and the worst dates. I've shared some of my most magical moments with you over a better part of the last decade.

And now, it's time to say goodbye. I have been meaning to write you a love song but I can't get myself to do it. I still have the occasional urge to kiss you and hold you from time to time, but for our sake, we should part ways. We have the power to seriously debilitate each other if we continue.

I wish you all the best. Thank you for everything. I will never find a love truer than yours. Ever.

#73: Hair Today, Gone Tomorrow

She wore a very pretty, pink, long-sleeved sweater that hugged her body and showed off her curves quite well. Her jeans were a couple of sizes too small, which was perfect for me, for obvious aesthetic reasons. She walked towards me from across the crowded bar, with a lovely smile on her lips – blood-red lips that broke into an easy smile that wrinkled the corners of her hazel eyes and made her look that much more beautiful. She was a little under 5'10" – tall, and easily one of the tallest women in the room.

She moved with a graceful, relaxed-yet-sexy walk, with her brown-streaked curls bouncing up and down with each step. She walked over to me; her smile widened as I stood up and hugged her tightly for a couple of seconds, and held out a chair for her. My fingers deliberately brushed her shoulders and her waist as I helped her into her seat, leaving no doubts in her mind what my intentions were.

"A gentleman," she said. "You guys are hard to find these days."

Her voice was sweetness personified. The lilting tones put my head into overdrive and even before I could say anything, I felt a stirring in my loins, an almost animalistic urge to pounce on her and take her roughly, right there in the crowded bar.

I smiled my best smile and said, "Then I'm glad you found me."

We spoke of this and that, made small talk, and flirted quite a bit. We ordered a couple of drinks and a bite to eat. I put my hand over hers and held it there for a few minutes. She didn't retract her hand. Instead, she locked her fingers between mine and we sat there, looking into each other's eyes. Was this love at first sight? Was I really doing this? Meeting this beautiful woman, holding her hand, looking into her eyes and steadily falling in love?

The waiter handed me the bill, and just as I was about to pay, she reached over and snatched the bill away from me.

"I'm paying," she said with a sweet smile.

I couldn't react because I had seen something that had sent a shiver down my spine and in an instant, filled my very soul with terror. I wish I hadn't seen it and I hoped I had imagined it, but I knew it was wishful thinking. I had seen the most terrifying sight that threatened to make me into a sniveling coward.

"Uh," I said. "Look, I – I have to go. I am running late for a meeting."

She stared at me confused, stunned, unable to comprehend. Even before she recovered, I stood up, hastily threw down some money on the table and muttered something about it being my treat, stammered an apology and like a fool, I stumbled out of the bar and ran for my life. I did not take a cab, I did not even bother looking for my bike that I had parked close by. I ran the three blocks to my house, in full sprint, not looking back. I was scared and I was not going to stop until I reached home.

After what seemed like an eternity, I reached my front door, out of breath and wheezing heavily. I rang the doorbell and almost collapsed into my roommate's arms. Being one of my closest friends, he was obviously shocked and worried. He helped me into a chair, gave me some water and helped me calm myself down. My kid sister, who was also home, came out of the room and stared at me. I looked a total mess. They asked me what happened and demanded an explanation. They even offered to call the cops, thinking I had been mugged.

"No, don't call the cops. They won't be able to do anything," I managed to say between deep breaths.

[181]

"Nikhil, you're scaring me," said my sister. "What happened!?"

I looked into their faces – my sister and my best friend – anxiously looking at me, waiting for an explanation. So, I told them the story about how I had met the perfect woman, the wonderful time we had had, the drinks and the dinner and the conversations. Then I reached the point in the story where the bill arrived and she had reached out to snatch it from my hand.

"What happened? Why did you run when she took the bill??" asked my roommate.

"Dude," I said. "She had body hair!"

#74: The Man From Nowhere

"See the nowhere crowd cry the nowhere tears of honor
Like twisted vines that grow
Hide and swallow mansions whole..."

– James Hetfield, *The Memory Remains*

He came from nowhere and he didn't know where he was headed. He seemed lost, confused, a paper boat caught in a hurricane, with turmoil eroding the last traces of sanity and reason in his head. He was escaping, hopefully to a better tomorrow, but he didn't know for sure. He wanted a fresh start, desperately. He didn't know how he was going to achieve it – his bad luck seemed to have followed him here as well. Everything he tried seemed to fail, and fail miserably. He caught himself searching for straws to clutch at.

He vowed to find a muse, an inspiration, a candle in the whirlwind of his bad luck. He wanted to find the elusive abundance of good luck that had deserted him for so long. He yearned for the peace and tranquility that had been hiding from him. It was not a search in vain.

He met her on a hot, sunny afternoon and they regarded each other cautiously, unsure of just how much attention the other person warranted. She seemed harmless enough, but he was expecting his seemingly unlimited quota of bad luck to step in again.

"Been a while," he said. Cautiously. Two tigers, one paranoid and the other indifferent, circling each other.

"Yes. How have you been?" she asked.

"Good," he replied and they went on to talk about other things mundane.

Time flew by and a pact was etched in stone between them, unwritten yet indelible. It took time, obviously. It did not happen overnight. He began to experience her presence more and more in his life until it almost became an addiction. Over time, he started craving for her company. She became the beacon of light in the darkness that had clouded him. She forced him to embrace good luck again, though he never knew how she managed to do that.

He still had no destination in mind, but he knew that his journey wouldn't be lonely anymore; the journey that had started from nowhere and had seemed to head nowhere; the journey that she had spectacularly derailed and made more bearable. He had a lot of things to be thankful for. And for a million things more.

He had found his muse. He had found his share of good fortune. The man from nowhere was finally home.

#75: Habit Over Hate

I've been living in a beach town for a while now and working for an ad agency, setting up a business of my own and working on my third book, so arguably, I've been a bit busy. Add an ill-timed illness and brand new fuckers around and it does get a bit dicey to manage time.

But anyway, here I am, itching to tell the world about my beach town.

For a while now, I've noticed that the town I live in has been mistakenly called many names and not all of them pleasant. It has been referred to as the *Crap Recycler, The Widowmaker, The Land of Opportunity* and, my favorite, *A Triumph of Habit Over Hate*.

I don't think it's any of those. The more I look at this town, the more I come to believe that it's a small-time beach town that has had a sudden influx of different dichotomies: randomly distributed pockets of wealth and penury, steel-and-concrete monstrosities and corrugated cardboard disguised as houses, intellectuals and dumbasses.

There are still remnants of the little beach town that it actually once was – the early morning air with the slight hint of seawater in it, the small lanes paved with tiles, thatched roof huts (if you're lucky enough to spot one), tall coconut trees and the stink of freshly caught seafood. People getting haircuts and shaves on the pavement, the constant cacophony of the crows (which seems to be a trait of almost every beach town), and finally, the vast areas of mangroves that signal the edge of land, all make up for a wonderfully misunderstood beach town.

Then there are the beaches themselves. Some beaches here have been overrun by people who, I think, have never seen a beach in their lives and hence empathize with. But others are pristine in their naturalness. Vast stretches of sandy shores devoid of any human pollution, the gentle lapping of the waves as they kiss your feet and the distant horizon where the unnaturally large sun sinks, throwing up a fascinating array of golden lights dancing on the rippling water.

There I go again, losing myself while describing the sea. The point I was trying to make is that all these things put together make this place a lovely little beach town which has all the beauty and serenity of any other place like Gokarna or even some parts of Goa, with all the amenities of a fully-developed city of money, power, cricket and Bollywood. It would help if we go past the negativity that is being spun into our lives by everyone who's been here. Four out of every five news reports in every newspaper is negative – murders, political scams, money laundering, government incapacities, road rage, traffic snarls, and other nonsense. Forget all that for a day. If you live where I live, try and overlook all that for just a day. Try and connect with the small-time beach town that it really is.

I live in Mumbai.

#76: Daydreaming

One of the worst things that could happen to anyone in my position is this: the realization that your daydream will not come true. At least not immediately. You're right up there among the stars, imagining how different your life will be and how you are going to spend the suitcase full of cash you just found on the sidewalk – a car each for yourself and your wife; maybe a new Harley for those exciting road trips on which, taking a car would be lame; a new house, perhaps two; a very strong and comprehensive health insurance plan for the entire family – yours and hers – to ensure that everyone who's important is taken care of; and some extra leftover money invested in low yield bonds, savings, deposits and other such inane piggy-banks to ensure your financial independence. Of course, you'd first pay off your credit cards and loans and become debt-free.

You and your wife would then quit your respective jobs. You'd move in to one of your new houses, make it a home and give out the other one on rent to a decent family to ensure that you get paid monthly. You consider this as your primary income which is earmarked for groceries, food and fuel. You then buy yourselves a pair of fancy smartphones that have the very latest features and you use these phones to tweet about how excited you are about what you're planning to do next.

Once the tweet has been published, you pack your bags and you hit the road to begin the longest journey of your life – a long road trip all over the country, on a quest to visit each and every state, drive on every road, experience all that the beautiful country has to offer. You'd spend almost a year on the road and you return to your new house (which is still new because you haven't lived in it yet) and you spend a few months domesticating yourselves. You do the occasional trip on the

Harley to a few places here and there that may have escaped your radar during the year-long road trip.

After about a year of domestic life, your wife starts getting restless and insists that you do something out of the ordinary. She wants that excitement of living out of her backpack again. She wants to drive into the sunset and sit on the hood of your big SUV, looking out at the setting sun and smoke a cigarette and drink a Diet Coke, while you stand next to her with your beer can in hand, lean over to you just as the last rays turn the sky red and kiss you softly on the lips. She urges you to do something about this urge.

You walk over to the window overlooking the beautifully landscaped garden in front and you think about what to do. You wake up the next day and decide to sell off your other house. You contact your lawyer and find out that the price of the house has nearly doubled in the two years since you bought it. You make the deal with the first buyer you find and a week later, you're richer by an insane amount of cold, hard cash, sitting pretty in your bank account. You spend a weekend researching the best way to spend a whole year backpacking in Europe. You make the arrangements, book your tickets and your hotels, and you go out on a Sunday evening to the mall and buy brand new backpacks and new travel accessories for yourself and your wife, and come back home in time for dinner. When your wife asks you where you were, you deflect the question innocently and move the conversation over to mundane things like the weather.

The next morning, you ride your Harley over to the bank and realize that you have far more money left over than you initially imagined. You then convert a lot of the money into Euros, a lot of the money into Dollars and a lot of the money into travelers' checks. You also instruct the bank to issue you a Visa travel card, into which you pre-load a lot of money.

You then go back home and tell your wife that you have something important to show her. She is confused, obviously. But curious. When you reveal your master plan and the preparations you've made so far, she is fantastically overjoyed and you get the best sex of your life for being the best husband ever.

[188]

You realize that you're in a public place and you have a hard-on. You quickly clear your mind, pull down the visor of your helmet, start your bike just as the light turns green, and continue the ride to your office.

#77: Indian Politics: A Cynical Deconstruction

Once upon a time, there was a whore who refused to take a bath. She was the largest whore in all the world. No other member of her profession could match her for size. She could single-handedly take on a gang of twenty men and still beat them all to a pulp with brute strength. She was widely known for her prowess and her surprisingly good heart, and everyone respected her. She wanted nothing more than to whore around and make money, something that she'd been doing for almost six decades now. The one thing no one liked about her was the fact that she didn't take a bath.

She used to take a bath in the past, some fifty years ago, but now, she just couldn't get herself to do it. She got used to carrying on her flesh trade using nothing more than deodorant. When she forgot the deodorant, her stink would announce her arrival five minutes in advance. Yet, she never had a dearth of customers. Buying her services gave people a sense of false pride, something that was an archaic notion in itself. People would line up to wait for her just to be able to spend a few precious moments with her, so that they could be branded with her stinking sigil. They would use it in their résumés, and their families would be proud of their achievements. The fact that they'd just participated in prostitution was never a problem. People didn't talk about the ethical, legal and moral quandaries of using the services of a whore. These things were swept under the carpets and the mattresses or locked in cabinets, never to be spoken of.

The whore who never took a bath had a certain reputation that she wasn't proud of: she had been the cause of more deaths in her country than any disease, calamity or natural disaster. She wielded her heavy hand as a weapon and swatted away anyone who dared to come forward to clean her. She used people's religious beliefs to get under their skin and convinced them to kill other people with different religious beliefs. In fact, her refusal to clean herself up was so notoriously known that even people in other countries were afraid to do anything lest they become scarred and soiled. The whore went on mercilessly killing innocent people in order to satisfy herself of her uncleanliness. A lot of people tried to clean her and were either soiled themselves or killed off as expendables.

Indian politics is, in one word, dirty.

#78: Hate & Why We Love It

I was reading a rather disturbing feature on *Time* about the attack on a guy called *Nido Taniam* in Delhi – he was attacked because he looked Chinese. It struck me that this, and other instances of hate that happen all over the world every day, are not surprising. We can't pretend to be shocked, awed and disturbed, and cringe away from these acts of violence. As human beings, we are programmed to inflict pain on others. And we love it.

My theory is quite simple: we are hateful creatures, forced to live together on the same piece of land with a bunch of makeshift rules and laws thrown in to govern our behavior. We forced ourselves into this corner. No one did this to us.

On our own, we are quite the pacifists. Well, most of us. But why is it that when we are put in a crowd of people, we bare our teeth, beat our chests and turn on each other? I think the answer lies deep within ourselves – our inherent fears. I'll explain what this means.

I've been doing a very interesting social experiment for a few years now without anyone realizing it, and it's proven to be quite the eye-opener. Whenever I am alone with someone (say Bob), in any situation, the conversation progresses like any other conversation between two people – about random things or about something in particular. The minute a third person (say Dave) joins the fray, I use a variation of the following line: "Dave, hey! What's up? Have you met Bob? He's my friend and he's uh.. um..."

I pretend to forget what Bob does for a living or what he's good at, or what he has achieved, in an attempt to trivialize him. Bob immediately takes the cue, subconsciously, and rattles off his résumé to Dave – where he studied, what he graduated in, where he has worked and what he is currently working on. This does not always happen, mind you. But when it does and you observe Bob's body language, and he is the very epitome of defensiveness. His body is closed, arms folded, shoulders drooped, as though he is bracing for an attack.

The same thing also happens when I'm alone with Bob and I feign indifference to his achievements in life.

It's our fear of rejection (or the fear of being dismissed as unimportant) that puts us in this situation. We all do it. I do it too. I have found myself talking about my career choices and my achievements (or lack thereof) to people for no fathomable reason except to mask my fear of ridicule and rejection. I don't want the other guy to think I'm weak. Or stupid. I beef up my arms and shoulders, brace myself and start telling him through my body language that I'm a (relatively) smart guy and can defend myself if need be.

This behavior tells us a few very important things about ourselves – we are all in a constant state of alertness, always on the lookout for a threat. This threat can be in any shape or form – physical, mental, emotional and financial. We believe that everyone around us are threats to our way of life. This is perhaps why we don't do certain things like wear sunglasses when we're indoors – we fear that people are going to point at us and laugh, thus making us feel small, insignificant and vulnerable. This leaves us open for attack from a larger predator.

When the concept is extrapolated globally – to societies and nations as a whole – we realize that the equation does not change one bit. A billion paranoid people are constantly wary of a billion other paranoid people. Fear multiples in crowds and takes a life of its own, which leads to bad decisions and ultimately, a lot of people die. This is used as fuel to further our paranoia – because it's all right when *we* kill someone because we are doing it out of self-defense. But we fail to realize that the other person is killing *for the same exact reason*. We think he's a monster, with no thought control and emotion.

The fact that we need this mutual hate and fear to survive and to lead our lives is the biggest illusion that we have performed on ourselves. The idea that we need to lash out at a fellow human being in order to survive is ultimately going to make us as extinct as the Dodo. But not before we realize that it makes us just as dumb.

#79: Pursuit Predators & Missing Airplanes

I stumbled as I ran blindly in the dark. The night seemed eerily quiet all around me except for the noise I made as I ran. When I stopped for breath, the pounding in my chest and my rapid deep breaths of panic were all I could hear. I couldn't perceive anything around me. As I ran ahead, all I could think of was to survive. And I needed to get back to my ship. I had to escape this hell.

I seemed to be in some kind of an overgrown jungle. Wet leaves, branches and fronds slapped me all over as I ran through them. I was thankful for my body suit but I was worried about my air filters. Through the foggy visor of my helmet, I peered down at my chest and saw that the air filter was choked with dirt. I brushed some of the dirt away awkwardly with my gloved fingers and immediately felt the cool rush of breathable air circulate inside my suit. I took a deep, satisfying breath and looked back at the dark jungle through which I had just run.

I could only see the dark silhouettes of the forest and the looming shadows of enormous trees, standing tall like black shadows of ancient giants against the dark night sky. A few smattering of stars here and there twinkled down at me, as if amused at my plight. I leaned against the trunk of a huge tree and took a few more deep breaths, calming my nerves. My legs trembled less and less with each passing second and I could feel my heart rate slowing down. I didn't hear the faint whizz of the metal spear but felt the sickening impact as it embedded itself with a dull *thunk* into the tree trunk, barely an inch from my hand. I jumped back, and ran. The creature had been following me and hunting me for over three hours now and it was showing no signs of giving up. Each time I thought I had put sufficient distance between us I was proved wrong. It was always near, lurking around the corners, hiding in the shadows and shooting its high velocity metal spears with a makeshift bow.

I cursed this planet as I ran. We should never have stopped here to explore. It was all Kai's fault. If only she had had half a brain. Well, she was dead now, killed by one of those deadly metal spears that had flown out of nowhere and had lodged itself firmly in her throat. I shook my head and forced myself to stop thinking about Kai. I was alone on an alien planet that was intent on killing me. I had to make my way back to the ship. That was my only hope. I dodged the forest left and right, high and low, retraced my steps to throw the creature off my track, and finally found a tree trunk that I could climb. It was high enough to hide me from being clearly visible. I thanked the darkness and climbed as high as I dared, hugged the branch and lay still, watching the forest floor beneath me. Every rustle of a leaf and every chirp of an insect seemed to reverberate in my ear. My senses were on hyper alert.

On the horizon, I could see faint snatches of light from various points, glowing over the tops of the trees. Far away in the distance, I thought I heard the whine and growl of machinery, but I couldn't be sure. We were told this was a primitive planet. We were told that life was almost impossible here due to the heavy, toxic atmosphere and the crushing gravitational pull of the nearest star. We were told to explore without fear and that it would be routine. I'd love to see the faces of those Command Center fucks now.

We were scientists. I was a specialist in alternative energy studies and my sole purpose on this trip was to collect geothermal readings from various planets, analyze them and rate them according to the ease of harvesting. In other words, I was a lab rat. Not a fucking soldier. I didn't know how to survive in these situations. These creatures were terrifying to say the least.

We first encountered the aliens four hours into our exploration. The landing was routine, without any incidents. Kai and I had strayed far from our ship, collecting samples and making small talk when the clearing in which we stood was doused in bright, harsh light that blinded us. The light seemed to emanate from the forest itself. I could see Kai panicking, screaming and I ran to her to calm her down. We

[196]

heard the guttural sounds that seemed to be a form of vocal communication. We looked up to see three figures walking towards us, gesturing and speaking. All I could make out was the unnaturally long limbs and the row of white, jagged teeth on their heads. I felt Kai shuddering suddenly in my arms and when I looked down, I saw the metal spear sticking out of her. I felt her body go limp. The creatures had killed her without warning. Without provocation. I ran.

I felt an insurmountable anger boil inside me as I lay on the tree branch. Anger at myself, at those short-sighted Command Center nuts and anger at these vile, merciless aliens and their makeshift weapons. I wanted to destroy it all.

I stiffened as I heard the rustle of the leaves somewhere to my left. It was different from the usual rustle of the wind. This was unnatural. I lay very still and saw the leaves part and the creature step forward slowly. It seemed to be looking at the floor, trying to discern my footprints. These types of pursuit predators were the scariest – they never tired, they never gave up and they hunted you down from your footprints and the twigs your feet snapped while you ran. The creature held the makeshift weapon in one hand as it slowly moved on two feet looking this way and that, and passed beneath my tree. I could see the top of its head as it passed under me. I was tempted to jump down and fight it, but held myself. I didn't know how many more of them were out there.

I looked around in the general direction of my intended escape. The ship was somewhere off to the right and from my vantage point here, I could faintly see the outline of the ship's tail. It was close. Closer than I thought! I felt a renewed surge of hope in me. I made sure that the creature was gone before I descended as quietly as I could and started jogging towards the ship. My heart skipped a beat when I heard the loud guttural shout from behind me. I didn't look back. I ran as fast as I could. I could hear two, three, four, countless creatures behind me, all shouting and crashing after me. Where did so many of them come from?

I felt a searing pain shoot through my arm and when I looked down, I almost fainted in fright. I saw a thin metallic spear stuck in my arm. It

[197]

had pierced the palm of my hand clean through! I didn't dare pull it out. The pain was excruciating. I felt loud bangs from behind and I ran as the forest exploded all around me. One moment there was a lean tree trunk and the next, a loud bang from behind and the tree trunk exploded in splinters that rained over me as I ran headlong into the forest. I prayed and prayed that I was going in the right direction. The noise behind me was deafening.

I ran through the pain in my hand. I could feel the numbness creeping up my arm from the point where the spear had pierced through. I felt faint but forced myself to keep running. Escape! That was the only thing on my mind.

After what seemed like an eternity and almost when I thought of giving up and surrendering to the aliens, I broke through the tree line and almost collided with my ship. I screamed out in ecstasy and agony and clambered around the hulking machine and into the open bay door at the back. I saw the aliens break through the tree line and stop as they saw the ship. Through the closing bay door, I saw them hesitate. They seemed to be awestruck at the sight of the ship. One of the aliens saw the bay door that was closing and caught sight of my face through the rapidly closing slit. The metal spear it fired pinged harmlessly off the ship and I heard the satisfying bangs and the thuds of the door closing and the bolts driving home.

I stumbled my way to the cockpit and hit the big red button on the dashboard. Everything would be automated now. The ship would take me home.

I slumped down on to the floor and looked at my hand. I could see the metal spear sticking out from both sides of my palm, firmly lodged. The ship trembled slightly as the fuel heated up and the ignition kicked in. I almost felt sorry for the alien creatures standing outside the ship. They would all be fried to nothingness in about ten seconds. It was a pity. I could have observed them and studied them, had it been under different circumstances. I thought I heard them scream as the ship fired on all cylinders and cooked them to a crisp and lifted off. I breathed a sigh of relief as it picked up speed. In about fifteen seconds, it would automatically open up the wormhole into our world and shoot into it. I could hardly wait to get home and get someone to pull this fucking spear out of my hand.

I stood up gingerly and saw out of the cockpit window at the fascinating landscape of the vast blue planet beneath me. An entire planet that had evolved to breathe the most corrosive gas in the universe – oxygen. I shuddered at the thought.

I saw the brilliant golden glow of the wormhole opening up in front of me. Just as the ship neared it, out of the corner of my eye, I saw some movement out on the horizon. The last thing I saw before being sucked into the wormhole was a huge metal cylinder hurtling through the air at a ferocious speed – almost like an aircraft – crashing into the ship at what seemed like a million miles per hour and the entirety of the fire and the debris being sucked into the wormhole. Drifting in the void of the wormhole, I saw the remains of the object that had collided with my ship. Hundreds and hundreds of those alien creatures floated away in the zero gravity of the wormhole, all dead. It couldn't have been an aircraft, I thought to myself. This was supposed to be a primitive planet. Someone is going to have a lovely time trying to find this plane, I thought, smiling to myself as I blacked out, and hoped at the back of my mind that my arm and all my thirty-one fingers would be intact.

Author's Note: This is based on a true story. No one's found the plane yet. My condolences to the families of the victims.

#80: The Misjudged Criminal

"This country has gone to the dogs!" muttered the mechanic as he bent over my shiny bike.

I stood behind him and said nothing, boiling in the unseasonably hot weather that seemed to force every drop of water out of my body as sweat. I glanced at my watch and realized I was getting late for work, and the traffic would have built up to an impenetrable mass of steel and smoke by now. Bangalore on a summer morning is not for the weak-hearted.

"You're lucky they didn't rip this whole thing off. It's a custom-made part and very expensive," he said and continued to tinker with the bike, crouched so low that he was almost squatting. I asked him to hurry up and told him that I was getting late for work.

One Year Earlier:

He knew he didn't do anything wrong. He hadn't meant to steal the diamond. He'd just found it lying on the floor next to the dead body, shining pretty in a pool of congealed blood. He'd picked it up, wiped it on his shirt and had tried his best to avoid looking at the corpse, which was stinking up the place a bit. Just as he had thanked his luck on finding a diamond as big as a golf ball, he heard the distinct sirens of an approaching police vehicle. He'd panicked and run in the wrong direction, almost directly in front of the two bright headlights that screeched to a halt. Two constables had jumped out, armed with their *lathis* and had yelled something at him. He hadn't paused to think. He had just run.

[200]

He thought back on his stupidity as he ran down the deserted roads of Bangalore, past the Navrang Theater. He could hear the running feet of the constables pursuing him, yelling at him to stop. They had probably just wanted to question him. He should have just stayed there and answered their questions. *Who am I kidding*, he thought bitterly. They would have just framed him for the murder, confiscated the stone from him and thrown him in jail to rot for the rest of his life. The cops in this city were notorious for their stupidity and laziness. *I did the right thing*, he thought, as he ran.

He picked up speed and decided to dodge the pursuers in the countless narrow alleyways that peppered the road on either side. His heart sank as he heard the sound of the siren at a distance behind him. The police jeep had joined the pursuit! He looked around and saw a half-open shutter of what looked like a motorbike service center. He didn't think – he ducked in and the darkness of the warehouse enveloped him. He could hear his heart racing madly as he stood still in the corner, in complete darkness, and worried that the cops would hear it too. He didn't move a muscle and stood there for a long time after the running constables and the police jeep had passed the warehouse. He didn't dare move and go out again. He felt around him and his fingers found a blanket hanging from a wall peg. He snatched it off and draped it around him. He could feel the bulk of the diamond pressing up against his thigh through his trouser pocket. He clutched it tightly and made a decision that he would regret for almost a year.

Yesterday:

Midnight found him walking alone, dejected, shoulder slumped, clutching a half-empty bottle of the local whiskey. His whole life had been a series of missed chances and unlucky coincidences that had almost ruined him once. He still shuddered a bit when he thought back to that fateful day a year ago when he had almost been caught for a murder that someone else had committed. Every now and then, his hand went to his thigh where the golf-ball sized diamond had poked him – in his darkest dreams, he dreamed that he had the diamond in his hands and was enjoying the wealth that it brought him. Not a day went by in which he kicked himself for hiding the stone in one of the parked motorbikes. The only thing he remembered was that it was an Avenger model. He had hid the stone in a crevice of the engine and stepped out of the warehouse to make sure the coast was clear. He didn't want to be caught with the stone in his possession in case a constable or two were canvassing the area. He had walked around slowly, ready to drop to the ground and pretend to be drunk and homeless at the first sight of a cop.

No one had been around. After about fifteen minutes of walking around, he had decided to chance it and had headed back to the warehouse to collect his precious diamond. He had stood in front of the warehouse, shaking in anger, cold, fear and the deepest despair, staring at the shutter that was now firmly closed and locked. In his panic, he had walked all around the building trying to find a way in, but in vain.

The next morning, he had been present at the warehouse door when it opened and barely had enough time to notice that the precious motorbike that held his diamond was a black Avenger 220 cc bike with the registration number ending with 9669, before he had been chased away by the security guard. He had taken up an all-day vigil across the street from the warehouse, waiting for the precious bike to be wheeled out. He had decided that he would take his chances in broad daylight and try to remove the diamond from its crevice. All his hopes had been dashed, however, by a fat man who rode off on the bike. He had stood there helplessly and seen as the fat man disappeared down the road, through an endless stream of tears in his eyes.

He stumbled and fell to the ground as he remembered that fateful day and let out a wail of despair. He cursed God and everything that he felt like cursing and crawled on all fours in the middle of the empty tree-lined street, with only his shadows and the harsh orange street lights for company. He crawled to the sidewalk and sat down heavily, taking a swig from his bottle. As he lifted his head to drink, he saw the goddamn bike parked across from him. *It was that bike!* It was a black Avenger 220 cc bike, numbers ending with 9669. He looked at it, his hand paused in midair and the whiskey pouring on his legs and onto the street, which he didn't notice. He stared at the bike for a good, long minute and looked around to see if there were anyone else on the road. He dropped the bottle and scrambled hastily on all fours across the street to the cursed bike, grunting with anticipation and pain. He crawled up to the bike and his hands trembled as he touched it. Tears welled up in his eyes, his lips quivered as he cried, this time in joy. He seized the strange-looking engine part with both hands and ripped it apart. He looked longingly at the little golf-ball sized diamond that fell out of the crevice and sat in his palms.

The engine part that he had ripped out, dangled from a few cables and wires, dripping petrol, oil and other fluids on the ground, and saw the man run away, whooping with joy and laughing hysterically.

Present Day:

"But why would anyone do that?" I asked, as I paid twenty rupees to the mechanic.

"Carburetors fetch anywhere between four hundred and five hundred rupees, sir," he said. You're lucky they didn't steal it. They were probably interrupted by someone."

"I guess so. Thanks," I said, climbed on to my bike, and rode to work. The thought of someone trying to steal my bike's carburetor angered me. The thought of negotiating the traffic in the heat of the summer put me in a bad mood. I just knew the day was going to be a long, bad one.

An Apology To End With

You have my congratulations if you have reached this page and not lost your sanity yet. Did I not warn you?

Anyway, I want to end this abomination with a sincere, heartfelt apology for what I've written. If I have hurt your feelings in any way or if I have inadvertently hit a nerve, or if I have done any one of a million things to cause you anger, pain, discomfort or constipation, I am sorry.

I wish you all the best in life and I hope you don't have to read any more bullshit like this. I mean it. If you are a member of the press and are reading this to review the book in your publication, I strongly encourage you to slander it. I will not feel bad. I deserve it.

If you are affiliated to Bollywood or Indian politics in any way, then I will not apologize to you. I will, only if you make a big deal out of it and talk about it on Arnab Goswami's News Hour.

Acknowledgements

This book would not have been possible if it weren't for the dedicated indifference of a lot of people who have been unspeakably supportive. I have used a lot of names in the book – some of them are real, some are not. If I have used your real name, then I probably have taken your permission. If I have not, then pretend it isn't you.

I would not have been able to write this book if it weren't for the constant support of my dear wife, Mansi Pal. I have driven her up the wall, forcing her to read and edit this pile of garbage so often that she's refusing to come down. She's a fantastic source of inspiration, makes a heavenly cup of tea and is my travel soul-mate. She travels with me and we write about our experiences at www.chaiaroundtheworld.com. Go ahead, read it.

My terrorist brother, Nitin Kumar, who's not really a terrorist, has been of great help in helping me choose the right adjectives, pejoratives and politically-correct slandering. He is the most creative writer I've known in my life and I hope he realizes it in time.

Some of the people I've mentioned in this book (either by their real name or their pseudonyms), who have been instrumental in the MirrorCracked journey by inspiring me to write at different times of my lives, are:

Vatson (the one who giggled), Scorpria (the one with the letters and the alphabets), Agonybeed (the one who got away), Chuckie (the one who's still around), Apar (the one who's always been there) and Divya (the one who's a mom now). Any of the women I've dated in the past and who've been mentioned here, either in passing or directly, are wonderful human beings who just had the misfortune of running into me. I apologize for the emotional scars and I hope you find it in your hearts to forget about me and move on. I'm married now.

I would be remiss in my duties if I don't thank the readers of MirrorCracked who have been, over the years, very nice to me and haven't turned me over to the cops. The bloggers from Chennai will always be special to me, not only because I love them for what they are, but because they ate my food and didn't complain.

Lastly, I want to thank you. Yes, you! The one who's bought the book and is reading this. You are a brave soul and there is greatness in your life.

Have a wonderful day and a fantastic life ahead.

Cheers!